There Goes My Social Life

THERE GOES MY SOCIAL LIFE

From Clueless to Conservative

STACEY DASH

with Nancy French

REGNERY
PUBLISHING
A Division of Salem Media Group

There Goes My Social Life is a work of nonfiction. Some names and identifying details have been changed.

Regnery® is a registered trademark of Salem Communications Holding Corporation

Cataloging-in-Publication data on file with the Library of Congress
ISBN 978-1-62157-413-2

Published in the United States by
Regnery Publishing
A Division of Salem Media Group
300 New Jersey Ave NW
Washington, DC 20001
www.Regnery.com

Manufactured in the United States of America

10 9 8 7 6 5 4 3 2 1

Books are available in quantity for promotional or premium use. For information on discounts and terms, please visit our website: www.Regnery.com.

Distributed to the trade by
Perseus Distribution
250 West 57th Street
New York, NY 10107

To my Uncle Ferdinand and my Grandmother Olga—
People who cared for me and encouraged me to go further
than I thought possible

CONTENTS

I have a fury in me that would lay waste to Hell.
I love madly with no bounds. My sorrow runs deeper
than the ocean. And...that fury gives me strength.
That love gives me courage and hope. That sorrow
brings me to my knees for wisdom.

—Stacey Dash

I AM!

I am—yet what I am none cares or knows;
My friends forsake me like a memory lost:
I am the self-consumer of my woes—
They rise and vanish in oblivious host,
Like shadows in love's frenzied stifled throes
And yet I am, and live—like vapours tossed

Into the nothingness of scorn and noise,
Into the living sea of waking dreams,
Where there is neither sense of life or joys,
But the vast shipwreck of my life's esteems;
Even the dearest that I loved the best
Are strange—nay, rather, stranger than the rest.

I long for scenes where man hath never trod
A place where woman never smiled or wept
There to abide with my Creator, God,
And sleep as I in childhood sweetly slept,
Untroubling and untroubled where I lie
The grass below—above the vaulted sky.

—John Clare

FOREWORD

BY SEAN HANNITY

I first met Stacey Dash after she was attacked just for expressing her support for Governor Mitt Romney's presidency. Her grace and class in response to unwarranted attacks really impressed me, and we've been friends ever since!

I knew she wasn't like many of the other conservative women I'd ever met. If you're involved in politics at all—or talking about it, like I am—you know what types of conversations usually come up. People are frustrated with the president, sick of Obamacare, fed up with the IRS scandal, worried about entitlements, scared about the ever-growing national debt, and pretty hopeless about the future of our nation.

That's why Stacey stood out.

Here's a woman who has never had one political science class. She's a half black, half Latino, 100 percent American who grew up in tough circumstances in the South Bronx, unconcerned about politics. This is something people like me have to face: politics is downstream from most people's normal lives.

That's why I love *There Goes My Social Life*. It is not a political treatise or a rant. It's just a story.

Her story is probably your story. No, you may not have been abandoned as a young child or ended up in a gang—yes, you read that correctly—but you probably have faced your own set of challenges and have found yourself disillusioned with the way the world works. Instead of looking to the government to help her get her footing, she got a job. You probably know by now that her job was acting and included being able to work with Bill Cosby, Richard Pryor, and Alicia Silverstone in the most iconic movie of the nineties.

But Stacey Dash is not Clueless. She began making observations about her country and politics that you may have also felt. Why is everything suddenly about race, when we are supposed to have been ushered into a post-racial world by this president? Why do a majority of black Americans vote for a party that seems to thwart their success? Why would society tell a black American woman to shut up just because she tweeted out support for a presidential candidate who wasn't a Democrat—which Stacey had the gall to do.

If you are a fan of the movie *Clueless*, I guarantee you this is not like any other Hollywood tale you've read. If you are a fan of Fox News, I guarantee you this is not like any political book you've read.

Ultimately, this is not a political or a Hollywood story, but is instead one woman's triumph over adversity through hard-earned conservative principles and a merciful faith.

Enjoy!

STARTING OUT LIFE IN THE SCHOOL OF HARD KNOCKS

I was three years old when I saw my first dead body.

I was walking to preschool—alone—looking to my left and right as I tried to make my way to the dilapidated building that housed my early education.

A, B, C, D . . . the teacher would say in a sing-songy voice. *Red, yellow, blue.*

I loved school—the crayons, the carpet squares, the plastic scissors with blunt tips—but I had to get there first.

It was a short walk, maybe five blocks, past the once elegant buildings that had long been abandoned, re-inhabited by squatters, and turned into shooting galleries. I didn't know what drugs were at the time, though they were all around me. In fact, it was drugs that had caused my parents—heroin and cocaine addicts—to leave me with another family who let me live with them for a few years. They gave me food and shelter, but did little else to protect me from the harsh realities of our neighborhood.

That's why I was meandering to school on my own that crisp autumn day. I looked up into the sky, above a building that had holes in the walls and boards where windows used to be. But when I got to an intersection, I happened to look down on the sidewalk, where I saw a boy, just a teenager, stuffed under a car.

I looked more closely.

His eyelids were open, and I glanced—just for a second—into his sightless eyes. I wished I hadn't. A chill ran over me. It was as if he was staring right at me. Brown skin, beautiful face, a short afro. Handsome.

Instead of running, I slowed my pace. The rest of the way to school I walked deliberately, past people still passed out from the night before, by a group of dogs who'd tipped over a garbage can, and over the filth of the streets that had accumulated for years. There was no reason to run, because there was nowhere to run. The air smelled vaguely like the unquenchable fires that were always burning because of arson, faulty wiring, and broken fire hydrants. In my entire time in that neighborhood I never—not even once—saw a police officer on my block.

The South Bronx would teach me many lessons that would shape the rest of my life—my relationships, my politics, and even my faith. My friends were the hustlers, hookers, and gang members who struggled in the face of futility, who sold drugs instead of living on food stamps, who settled matters with fists, knives, and guns because it seemed their only option, who stood tall against broken promises, who chose to be mad rather than sad. Some died violently, some rose above it, most muddled through life with dashed dreams thinly veiled by bravado and pride.

Their story is my story.

It's hard for some to imagine that a Fox News contributor, a—gasp!—Republican could come out of such circumstances. But what I've found is this. The school of hard knocks tends to teach you lessons in conservatism. As Irving Kristol famously said, a new conservative is just "a liberal who has been mugged by reality."

Well, over the course of my life, I've been mugged a lot.

I never went to college and couldn't tell you about the philosophy of Edmund Burke. But I have seen—over and over and over—the way liberal policies and conservative principles play out in the real, unforgiving world.

In a way, I wanted to write a book to bear witness to my neighborhood, to my friends who've died, to my family members who've been put in jail, to my buddies who never could quite fight their way out of the tragically flawed system that is derisively called "the ghetto."

There is a better way. Black people have the chance, the abilities, and the responsibility to take advantage of the amazing opportunities afforded by this nation.

That's why I'm telling my story. Amidst all the heated racial rhetoric and the divisive language that flows from the television, the Internet, self-appointed black spokespeople, and even our president, I want to take a moment and challenge the deeply held beliefs of my brothers and sisters. I want to speak out and say something true about race, politics, and America.

My whole journey in speaking out about issues that matter to me started back in 2012, with one little tweet.

ONE

THE TWEET THAT CHANGED MY LIFE

You have enemies? Good. That means you've
stood up for something, sometime in your life.
—Winston Churchill

I drove my BMW into the parking lot of St. Victor's Church and looked in the rearview mirror to apply my lipstick. Chanel lip cream, in the shade of "Coquette," which I've used ever since I learned about it from a makeup artist on one of the sets I've worked on over the years. I checked out my lips in the mirror, stuck the lip color back into my purse, jumped out of the car, and looked back at my parking job. A little too close to the line, I thought. That's when I noticed the worn bumper sticker that had faded in the California sun over the past four years.

Obama '08.

I sighed, headed across the small parking lot, and pulled open the heavy doors of the church.

I'd been "blacked" into voting for President Obama, I thought as I walked into the church. It was darker inside than it was outside, because the church was lit only by candles. While my eyes adjusted, I inhaled deeply the aroma: frankincense, the sweet, honeyed smell that I now associate with God Himself. The church was empty except for one or two other souls who'd come in for prayers.

I quietly walked over to the bank of votive candles, whose light was dancing on the wall behind them, and lit one for myself. In Catholic tradition, people often light a candle as they pray a specific prayer.

That's why I'd come.

Feeling adrift and a little nervous as I lit the candle, I got down on my knees and talked to God. It was October and the country was in a hotly contested presidential election. President Barack Obama was running against Republican challenger Mitt Romney, and election news dominated every television channel, every newspaper, every bumper. In California, the bumpers were pretty united for Obama... including mine.

But I had begun to disagree with my own bumper sticker. To be honest, I didn't know anything about Obama when I voted for him the first time. Like many other Americans, I looked at him, wanted America to be great, and pulled the lever.

Naive.

I needed to pray.

"God," I said. "Should I do it?"

Whether anyone's ever prayed about sending a tweet before, I don't know. But I had composed a tweet before leaving for church and just couldn't decide whether to send it.

I'd never gotten political, which is why Gina—originally my personal assistant, now my friend and even my sister—was against it.

"Don't do it," she advised. "Stay away from getting people angry. You're not known for politics, so there's no reason to get half of America mad at you."

But I had grown so tired of President Obama's shtick.

He had the opportunity to unite this country in such a profound way, but instead he did the opposite. When he accepted the Democratic nomination for president, I had so much hope. I was so sick of people complaining about race, prejudice, and bigotry—I feel like my whole life has been dominated by those kinds of accusations. I was ready for a black president who— once and for all—would prove that America had moved past its history of slavery and repression. If a black man could lead the free world, surely we as Americans had evolved into something better.

He sounded good.

"I am absolutely certain that generations from now, we will be able to look back and tell our children that this was the moment when we began to provide care for the sick and good jobs to the jobless; this was the moment when the rise of the oceans began to slow and our planet began to heal; this was the moment when we ended a war and secured our nation and restored our image as the last, best hope on Earth," he had said with such grandeur. "This was the moment—this was the time—when we came together to remake this great nation so that it may always reflect our very best selves, and our highest ideals."

In retrospect, I felt like a fool for actually believing that shit. A mere man was going to make the oceans recede? Please.

He couldn't even make good on his promise to cause America to "come together." We were more divided, angrier, and more partisan than I've ever seen in my lifetime. In fact, since Obama had taken office, suddenly everything was about race.

I hadn't paid too much attention to the last campaign. But any casual observer could tell, Obama was taking advantage of uneducated people by betting on one single fact: people would vote for him because his skin color was enough.

Black people agreed. More than once, I heard this sentiment amongst my black friends: Let's vote for him. He's black. It's enough.

My white friends agreed. Let's give him a break, they said. He's black. It's enough.

When he was elected, everyone was so excited. I remember his inauguration, when I gathered with friends to watch the momentous occasion . . . when suddenly—finally!—we were united.

I have to admit a tear came to my eye when I watched Barack Obama being inaugurated.

But when he actually took office, the soaring speeches faded a bit into our memory. We had to look at what he actually was doing instead of what he was saying…and it was a harsh reality check.

For the first time in American history, people wondered if their kids would be better off than they had been. In fact, President Obama seemed to have contempt for successful people. His 2012 challenger, Mitt Romney, was a successful businessman. But instead of acknowledging Romney's success, Obama seemed to hold it against him. Weirdly, the president held his opponent's success out as a reason for blacks *not* to vote for him.

He's not one of us, Obama seemed to be saying with every snide remark. He's just a rich white guy.

Of course, Obama—who had made millions off his books and other investments—wasn't really "one of us" either. But his skin camouflaged his Ivy League pedigree and liberal elitism.

His skin, however, wasn't enough to hide the economic realities we were all faced with—at the gas pump and when we got our ever-dwindling paychecks back. President Obama was doing a terrible job. In fact, he was leading our nation in the worst economic recovery since the Great Depression.

I wanted someone—anyone—to address the elephant in the room. I wanted someone to point out that skin color—no matter how pigmented—is not a qualification to be president of the United States of America.

Romney, on the other hand, had a resume that deserved respect. He had turned Massachusetts around when he was governor. He was obviously a good family man with a loving wife and a solid family.

I was at my home when he and Ann appeared on *Meet the Press* with David Gregory, and their message resonated with me. Ann responded to the constant criticism that her husband was out of touch because of his wealth by saying, "Mitt and I do recognize that we have not had a financial struggle in our lives, but I want people to believe in their hearts that we know what it is like to struggle. And our struggles have not been financial, but they've been with health and with difficulties in…different things in life."

I loved how Ann defended her husband against all the attacks. I loved how she and Governor Romney spoke about the need to move forward.

I was sick and tired of the accusations against the man. He was a businessman. That's what we needed.

I looked at the Twitter app on my phone and read the tweet I had written—but not sent—that morning before I left for church.

Vote for Romney. The only choice for your future. @mittromney @teamromney #mittromney #VOTE #voteromney

"Should I send this?" I prayed, and tried to quiet my mind. As the lady who'd been praying near the front of church shuffled by, I picked up my phone. The blue rectangular button at the top of my phone read, "tweet"—which is exactly what I did. In sending that tweet, I was going against the beliefs of 96 percent of black women in the country. But I've never gone with the flow. I had to take a stand, I thought.

A few hours later, I woke up from a Sunday afternoon nap, turned over in my bed, and turned on my laptop.

"Oh my God," I said. Normally, when I logged into Twitter, I'd see a few tweets and mentions. People would say something about one of my movies. Someone might ask about my life now. But now my Twitter feed was brimming with notes and messages.

Had I hit upon an enormous Romney-supporting demographic in Hollywood?

> i unfollowed stacey dash dumb ass

That's how the first tweet read. Hum. So I guess you win some, you lose some. Everyone's entitled to an opinion.

> so Stacey Dash supports Shitty Mitty…more power to her.

That was a bit better, I guess. But as I scrolled down my feed, I realized the reactions were overwhelmingly critical.

> I'm just going to hope that Stacy Dash (@REALStaceyDash) has had her Twitter account hacked…

> Stacey Dash need to start coppin pleas ASAP.. say she was hacked, popped a Molly something

> @REALStaceyDash just want attention because your career is played out.

An to think u were my favorite masturbation fantasy as a child @REALStaceyDash. I'm so disappointed in you!

Shut up bitch.

There was a time when I would walk through fire for @REALStaceyDash Now I wanna throw her in a volcano

Bitch, you rich. Fuck them n-ggers.

@REALStaceyDash…. …..how can u..as a woman…. support Romney? All racial issues aside…

@ guess u didnt read the black bible

Doesn't matter one way or the other. Stacey Dash is irrelevant…and has been irrelevant for SOME TIME NOW.

There were several that wished me death by suicide…oddly, the sentiment was always the same, but the spelling and capitalization wildly varied:

kill yourself
Kill urself!
Kill yourself
Kill yo self

Others got personal. Really personal.

This hurts but you a Romney lover and you slutting yourself to the white man only proves why no black man married u @REALStaceyDash.

She's an indoor slave. You know that Sis. You ready to head back to the fields, jiggaboo?

Stacey Dash has probably been thinking she's white since her Clueless days. All the signs were there.

So Stacey Dash buck tooth ass really voting for Romney!! Bitch, you black and Mexican...do yo think yo bloodline gone survive or something

The famous actor Samuel L. Jackson even piled on.

Wait, did Stacey Dash Really endorse Romney today?! REALLY????! Is she CRA..........??!

I pulled the covers up to my chin. My home was located in Studio City, a neighborhood in Los Angeles named after an old 1927 studio lot. The San Fernando Valley has been home to many celebrities, such as Ed Asner, Ryan Gosling, George Clooney, and William Shatner. My home was tucked safely behind gates and was very private, but I could hear the wind blowing through the bamboo trees I had planted outside my window for privacy.

The autumn afternoon sun poured in through the window, warming the room that suddenly felt cold. I got up and lit the logs in my fireplace before sitting back down and reading more messages.

The more I read them, the angrier I got.

"Don't read it anymore," Gina said. "It's not good for you!"

What had I done?

The vibration of my phone snapped me out of my reverie.

"You okay?" I heard on the other end of the line.

My attorney, Darcy.

"People are calling me Uncle Tom. Oreo Cookie," I said.

"Tell them to come up with something you haven't heard before."

It was true. Over the course of my life, I've been called every racial slur, I've been insulted, I've been mocked. But this?

"I'm used to criticism, but I can't believe how...*much* there is," I said.

"You're 'man bites dog.'"

"What'd you just call me?"

"You've heard of that phrase," Darcy said. "It just means that unusual events will get more attention than ordinary occurrences."

"What's unusual about someone talking about the presidential race during campaign season?"

"If a black woman had tweeted out support for Obama, that's 'dog bites man,'" she said. "No big deal. But a black woman tweeting support for a Republican against America's first black president?"

Darcy paused, so I filled in the blank for her.

"'Man bites dog.'"

"You got it."

I tucked the phone between my shoulder and my ear and reopened my laptop. I clicked on the notifications tab on Twitter and watched in awe as the tweets kept coming and coming.

"They're saying that I'm just doing this for the publicity," I said.

"That's actually why I'm calling," she said. "My phone's been ringing off the hook. Everyone wants you on their show—Fox News, Piers Morgan, *The View*, *Good Morning America*, everyone."

"But I *didn't* do this for the publicity," I said.

"I know," she said. "But the media wants to hear from you. They want to understand."

"They shouldn't have to 'understand.' Hell, look at the state of this nation. Voting for the other guy is not the most unimaginable thing. It's only because I'm black."

"We've established that, Stacey."

"But we haven't *established* that this is absurd," I said.

The phone was silent for a moment, and I was too mad to apologize. "What do you think I should do?"

"Pick one show, go on there and explain yourself, and be done with it," she said. "You'll get your opinion out there even more and you'll insulate yourself from the criticism of being a media whore."

"I think you're the only one who called me a whore."

"You apparently haven't read all of your Twitter feed."

I couldn't help myself. I laughed at that one.

"You can lead a whore to culture," I laughed, quoting Dorothy Parker. "But you can't make her think."

My Twitter feed continued to light up the entire week. The next day, Sandra Fluke—a Georgetown law student (now an attorney and women's rights activist) whom Rush Limbaugh had made famous when he called her a "slut" for demanding free contraception—tweeted out support for me.

> So disappointed to see people attacking @REALStacey
> Dash for voicing her opinion. Disagree politically, but
> #racist attacks are unacceptable.

I was criticized by people I didn't think would criticize me—including my former co-star Vivica A. Fox, who said my endorsement wasn't done "with class." But on the other hand, I got support from places I never imagined. On *The View*—not known for being hospitable to conservatives—Whoopi Goldberg defended me.

"She's entitled—and she's a nice girl…this isn't someone who went out and killed somebody. What the hell you people sending her crap like this for?!"

That's when the matriarch of *The View*, Barbara Walters, spoke up to try to explain the backlash.

"The reason she is being attacked is because she is black and the feeling is black people should not be voting for Romney," she said.

But Whoopi, God love her, wouldn't have it.

"Barbara," she said softly.

"Whoopi," Barbara replied.

"She is being attacked because she has a different view from other people," Whoopi said. "And I think you don't like somebody's views, that's okay, but to hand somebody death threats because…what the hell! What's wrong with us that this is what we do?"

I'll love Whoopi forever because of her strong, true words.

The excitement continued. One afternoon, I was sitting in my home, trying to deal with all of the Internet backlash. I decided to fight back on Twitter. It's not like me to sit back and let people talk shit.

It's my humble opinion…. EVERYONE is entitled to one

I tweeted. Then, I selectively responded to some of the snarky comments in my feed.

Later, I got a phone call from a number that wasn't already put in my phone. Thankfully, Darcy had given me a heads up.

"Hello?"

"Stacey, this is Paul Ryan."

My heart raced. I was talking to—hopefully—the next vice president of the United States. Ryan, of course, was the young— and I have to add hot—running mate on the Republican ticket.

"I just wanted to call and thank you so much for your support," he said.

"It's caused a lot of excitement," I said.

"Yes, I'm really sorry about the backlash," he said. "I actually can't believe the hate you are getting."

"Oh, it's okay," I said. "I'm used to it. Mainly, I want people to know I believe in what you're doing. I love your plan."

"Well, we just want you to know that we believe you're brave, and we support you," he told me.

"I just want our country back," I said. "And I hope you are able to do that."

When I put down the phone, I couldn't have felt better about my choice. The Romney/Ryan ticket was classy, kind, and lovely. Plus, they knew a thing or two about creating jobs. I decided to sit down and write out my thoughts more completely for my blog:

> I am an American citizen, who exercised her first Amendment right.
>
> I am self realized and believe that hard work and faith will allow me to achieve my American dream.
>
> I believe that Governor Mitt Romney believes in the American people. That we can be self evident, that we are capable of achieving the American dream. That there is enough for everyone. I believe that because he has proven his ability to lead, and his ability to be excellent as a CEO and as the Governor of Massachusetts. Governor Romney is the best choice to be our next President. He has achieved the American dream, he knows how to lead us the American people to

realize our potential. By creating 12 million jobs, giving equal work for equal pay, by giving incentives and cutting loopholes, by keeping us safe and strong as a country of Super Power. Yes, it is true, he is rich. So what better person to lead us to economic prosperity than someone who has attained it.

I believe that his faith and strong moral character will serve him very well as he Leads us to being the great United States of America we can be.

And so the saga continued. Online, on television, and around kitchen tables across America. I wanted to settle it once and for all. I didn't want my life dominated by politics or racial tweets. I wanted to have a normal life.

I believed one step toward normalizing my life again was to do one definitive television show. I chose Piers Morgan's show, because I'd always thought he was charming. (I guess I—like most Americans—have a thing for British accents.) As I packed my bags, I knew I wanted to take Gina. But the simple fact of the matter was that I couldn't afford her airfare.

Some of the tweets were saying I was "washed up" and irrelevant. I had to face facts. They weren't far from the truth. I'd had a great career. Most notably, I was in the now classic Alicia Silverstone film *Clueless* as Dionne, a character, like her friend Cher, "named after great singers of the past who now do infomercials."

But since that great role, I had made a few bad decisions. Actually, a lot of bad decisions, almost all because of men. My career had suffered, and my life had suffered. Actually, I'd just gone through a pretty terrible breakup when I sent that tweet.

It was okay. I was used to doing things alone.

I gave Gina a hug good-bye and headed to New York by myself. I might not have known a ton about politics, but I was sick of people saying that black people have to act in a certain way. I considered this more of an all-encompassing issue. This was about life.

As I walked onto the set of the Piers Morgan show, I was excited to finally be able to speak out.

"Joining me now, possibly the most controversial woman in America right now. She had the audacity as a black actress to vote for Mitt Romney," Piers said. "Can you believe that?"

I smiled at his obvious tongue-in-cheek introduction.

"She's never been known particularly for her politics but she is now. And it's all because of one tweet.... When I read about this, I felt offended for you," he said, ".... the idea that you as a black actress would come under such venomous attack...is extremely objectionable."

Piers asked me a series of questions—whether I was offended by the tweets, whether I thought the outrage was due to my color or my occupation, and—most important—why I had changed from supporting Barack Obama to Mitt Romney.

"I would say because of the state of the country and I want the next four years to be different. And I believe him.... I watched him, the governor and his wife on *Meet the Press*...they spoke to me and they seemed authentic and genuine."

"I really don't understand the fury," I said. "I don't under-stand it. I don't get it."

"Were you shocked? Were you saddened?" he asked.

"I am. I am shocked. Sad, not angry. Saddened and shocked…" I said. "But you know what, you can't expect everyone to agree with you."

The interview was fun, light, and I got across all of the points I'd hoped to convey. Plus, my Twitter followers skyrocketed, an added bonus. All in all, I was glad to put that chapter of my life behind me and get on with life.

Life, as it would have it, was about to get interesting.

Since I was in New York, I called my friend, hip-hop mag-nate Russell Simmons.

"Want to hang out?"

Within minutes, he rolled up in his jet black Maybach.

"Get in," he said.

TWO

THE PRETENTIOUS UNPRETENTIOUS

If I am not for myself, who will be for me? And when I am for myself, then what am "I"? And if not now, when?

—Hillel the Elder

'd never been in a Maybach before and was amazed at how much room was in the back.

"This is bigger than some Manhattan apartments," I said as I settled in. There was a cooler in the console, brimming with drinks.

Russell was a co-founder of Def Jam Recordings—and a founding father of hip-hop. He helped power the Beastie Boys, Run DMC, Public Enemy, and LL Cool J to stardom. But as successful as Def Jam was, it was just the beginning of his hip-hop empire. He also started a clothing company, produced television shows, had a management company, ran a magazine, and even began an advertising agency.

He offered me a drink, which I readily took. It had been one hell of a day, but he wasn't ready for small talk.

"So, you've been shilling for Money Mitt?"

"I was on *Piers Morgan Tonight*, if that's what you mean, but I'm hardly 'shilling.'"

"What do you call it?"

"Free speech?" I said.

"I guess technically you're free to support someone who couldn't care less about 47 percent of our country?"

"That 47 percent would be better off with a President Romney," I said. "Plus, you know Obama's full of shit."

"You can't say that," he said. "You're black."

"What does that have to do with anything?"

"And why'd you bring that fur coat in my car?"

"It's New York in October," I said, looking out the window at the well-heeled women walking on the streets of Manhattan. "I'm hardly the only one."

"You know I was PETA's person of the year, don't you?"

"I'm not going to be cold," I said, "because you want to pretend to give a fuck about a fox. You don't give a shit!"

I could faintly hear Russell's driver stifle a snicker. I bet he doesn't often hear anyone talk to Russell in this way. I didn't care if he was rich as hell. I'd known him for years, since back when he lived in Queens…before he was a yoga master, a vegan, or a mogul. I'd known him my whole life, and I wasn't going to put up with his shit.

"I guess you're gonna tell me you're still hunting?"

"Only pheasants," I said.

"Stacey, you know it's not right to kill those animals."

"And what are these seats made of?" I said, running my hand over the cool leather.

He threw his head back and laughed heartily. "You always have a way of turning things around."

The driver pulled up to the front of a beautiful bar that was reminiscent of a 1920s speakeasy. The ceilings were high, and the lights from the chandelier twinkled off the worn bar's mirror and bounced off the cocktail glasses in the hands of well-manicured patrons.

I walked in ahead of Russell, who stopped to give his driver instructions. Immediately, I heard, "Oh my God! Stacey Dash!"

There, seated with a friend, was Kristen Wiig—the talented and funny actress made famous by *Saturday Night Live*.

"I love you," she said, standing up to greet me.

"No, no, no," I said. "I love you!"

Before I could tell her how much I enjoyed her work on television and film, she was literally bowing down to me.

"You're the best," she said.

"No," I said. "You are."

"What kind of love fest am I interrupting?" Russell said as he walked in and saw us chatting. "Kristen, you'll have to join us."

After she sat down next to Russell and two of his girlfriends, he steered the conversation to politics. "Did your new friend Stacey tell you she was in town to promote Mitt Romney?"

Russell couldn't help himself. "Yeah, she's been busy on Twitter telling everyone that Obama needs to be fired."

"Wait," Kristen said, putting her hand up. "I love Stacey Dash, I don't want to hear you making fun of her."

Russell's two friends laughed.

"Why are you bringing this up," I demanded, "in front of people I just met?"

"Yeah, leave us alone," Kristen laughed. "We're sitting here talking girl stuff in our mutual adoration society."

I had a great time with Kristen, until we departed to head out to another venue. When our driver pulled onto 11th Avenue in Chelsea, I realized we were heading to the legendary Bungalow 8. This exclusive club—a frequent hangout for celebrities—was marked outside the door only with a neon sign flashing, "No Vacancy." The sign was meant to camouflage the club. This was not a place you happen to walk by and decide to pop in. This was for people in the know, and just a subset of those people. The line outside the door indicated that the club was hard to get into, so the sign took on a different meaning.

The guy at the door held people in the line back, judging their clothes and appearance with a tilted head. You could tell it was more than a job for him. Supposedly, he knew every person who walked through that door, and could tell you what everyone was wearing the last time they dared to enter...no matter how long it had been.

"Sorry folks," I overheard him say to a couple of well-dressed women as we cruised by. "No more room tonight."

This place was popular because lots of stuff went down here. You may have heard the rumors about Bungalow 8. This is where you might see Lindsay Lohan get too frisky on the dance floor or Paris Hilton bursting into tears on her cell phone. If a celeb had too much to drink, Bungalow 8 wouldn't necessarily call a cab. Instead, they might arrange for him or her to leave via helicopter from the helipad they had on top of the roof.

I know this was supposed to impress me, but seriously...who gives a shit?

We were whisked past the ropes and the lines of perfumed people. Russell smiled at the guy at the door without stopping. The club was decorated with potted palm trees, zebra-striped couches, and sparkly disco balls. The walls were painted yellow, patterned after the Beverly Hills Hotel. Apparently photography was forbidden—what happened at Bungalow 8 was supposed to stay at Bungalow 8. The club owners treated their celebrities with the ultimate discretion, so that it felt like old Hollywood.

The stars were out that night. At the first table full of people, George Clooney was holding court—telling stories and making everyone laugh. We joined them, including several other celebrities, and chatted and danced to Donna Summer songs.

"Anyone seen anything good on Twitter lately?" George said. Everyone started giggling behind their hands and then laughing outright.

I shot him a glance, but I realized he was just joking with me. The *New York Times* reporter who happened to be there didn't understand gentle trash-talking.

"So you're not willing to explain why you support Mitt?" the writer followed up, after I didn't take the bait.

"Yeah, I tweeted my support of Romney," I said, "And then I went on to *Piers Morgan* and backed it up. If you'd like to Google it you can see for yourself."

"But why?" he asked again.

"No, no, no," I said. "I'm not having this conversation here."

"She'd rather be having it out in a deer stand," Russell said. "She's a big hunter, you know."

"Did you kill that thing you're wearing right now?" the reporter asked.

"If you're asking if I believe in hunting and the Second Amendment," I said. "Then, yes, I do." I noticed the DJ had finally stopped playing 70s music and switched to top 40. I would've rather gone out on the dance floor at that moment, but I was being grilled.

"Like, in the same way the NRA does?"

I scrolled through the photos on my iPhone. I found one of me at my ex's ranch out west, holding up a pheasant. "Does this answer your question?"

"That literally makes me want to puke," Russell said, which made me laugh.

"I like to hunt, I wear fur, I don't believe in welfare, I don't believe in the NAACP, and I don't believe in the Muslim Brotherhood," I said, my voice rising. "What else do you think is wrong with me? Let's get it all out."

"I just don't get it," Russell said, pouring me more champagne.

"What's not to get?" I said, beginning to feel exasperated. Up until this point, I had managed to answer the questions easily without getting too offended. But by this time, it was feeling personal, like they had cornered me. Russell was saying, "How could you support a guy who wants to turn the cabinet room into a board room and sell America off to his rich friends? All the while, he's stashing their money in offshore bank accounts."

If this were in church, you would've heard some amens. But since it was in a bar in Chelsea, people just looked baffled as Russell continued.

"He's a guy who hasn't told the truth to the American people about where he stands on the important issues and will turn back equality for women, blacks, Latinos, and gays. I could certainly go on and on."

"You actually have been going on and on," I said. "Ever since I got in your fucking car."

"All I want to say is that Money Mitt works for the corporations."

"Your arguments are all bullshit…and half of America agrees with me," I said. "Tax breaks will entice the rich to invest in this economy and privatizing the social services like healthcare, education, and even social security will make it competitive, making them more responsible."

At this everyone just laughed, as if I'd made a joke. We'd had too many drinks to have a serious discussion.

"Wait, wait, wait," I said. "Aren't you worth over $300 million? Suddenly, you're angry at other people who have made it?"

"Because I'm rich, I can't have opinions?"

"You can't try to discredit Mitt, when you might actually be richer than he is," I said. "At least before you started bankrolling Obama's campaign?"

"She's got you there," George said. At this, the table erupted with laughter. Everyone knew "Uncle Russ" was rich as hell, and I think George loved seeing me put Russell in his place.

"I'm not having a political conversation with a bunch of drunks," I said, as I tipped back my flute. "Me included."

It was a challenging night—filled with arguing and accusations. But I was used to it. In *Clueless*, I had a line that always caused laughter in the theaters. My character Dionne is waiting to play tennis, when a classmate complains about having to participate in the athletic activities in phys ed.

"My plastic surgeon says to avoid activities where balls fly at your face," she complains.

"There goes your social life," I quip. I've always loved the script of that movie, and that was my favorite line by far. To this day, fans come up to me, say that line, and it cracks me up.

In a way, as I sat there with my friends, I felt that sentiment.

Dare to speak out about a hotly contested presidential election? When you're black? When you're an actress? When you're a woman?

There goes your social life.

My evening was a perfect demonstration of how hard it is for one side to really understand the other. I think Hollywood feels more comfortable welcoming directors who are accused pedophiles, famous actresses who are also thieves, boxers who are convicted rapists, directors who push cocaine, rappers who sell heroin, singers who solicit prostitutes, and actors who beat up their women than a Republican into their midst. In fact, people who fit into those categories still enjoy the professional adoration of their peers in Hollywood, even amidst the suspicion and guilt. It's like the only thing that can really ruin your reputation as a celebrity is to come out as a Republican.

Why does liberalism have such a stranglehold on Hollywood?

Because literally everyone they know is just like them. For all their talk of "diversity," the people in Hollywood only like diversity if it's skin-deep. They love to create friend groups that include blacks, whites, different ethnicities, and gays. But if the "diversity" extends to anything more than sexual preferences and skin color, they don't know what to do. The "diversity" in Hollywood is the easy kind—getting along with people who think and act exactly like you. That's why they didn't know how to categorize me when I spoke out against their deeply held beliefs. They like easy-to-digest "diversity," and I was making them think.

Yes, there are exceptions. But you can name secret—or in a few cases, not-so-secret—conservatives on two hands. Republicans have a few Hollywood stars—Clint Eastwood, Dwayne Johnson, Donald Trump, Adam Sandler, Jon Voight, Gene Simmons, Vince Vaughn, Patricia Heaton, Bruce Willis, and Stephen fucking Baldwin. Democrats have just about everyone else.

Like, everyone.

Democratic donors include Sting, Madonna, Alec Baldwin, Cameron Diaz, Matt Damon, Tom Hanks, and Bruce Springsteen. In 2011, celebs including Will Smith, Jack Black, Eva Longoria,

Magic Johnson, Quincy Jones, and Danny DeVito attended a $35,800-per-plate fundraiser for Obama. At the Soul Train Awards, Jamie Foxx got so drunk on Obama's Kool-Aid that he called the president "our lord and savior."

Not to be outdone, comedian Chris Rock came out and said, "I am just here to support the President of the United States. President of the United States is, you know, our boss. He's also, you know, the president and the first lady are kinda like the mom and the dad of the country and when your dad says something, you listen."

I think Chris may have skipped a few civics lessons. In a self-governing society, the people are the "boss" of the so-called political leadership. There's a reason why the office is one of "president" and not "king." Or "dad," I suppose.

Russell, of course, was all in for Obama too. He designed a shirt for Obama's campaign in 2008 and another in 2012. He hosted fundraising events, tweeted out support, and advocated for the campaign. Right before the election, he hosted a mixtape called *Yes We Can* (you can't make this shit up) featuring Talib Kweli, Kanye West, Wale, Busta Rhymes, and others. Hollywood's richest director, Steven Spielberg, donated $100,000 to the Obama campaign. Sarah Jessica Parker and Anna Wintour co-hosted a fundraiser for him in the West Village. DreamWorks Animation CEO Jeffrey Katzenberg donated $2 million to an Obama Super PAC; Bill Maher donated $1 million; Harvey Weinstein was one of Obama's biggest bundlers.

I have no idea how they can actually criticize Mitt for being wealthy, but they somehow managed to do it with a straight face.

In fact, I'd say the "Hollywood elite" like the people sitting at Bungalow 8 that night were Obama's main weapon in 2012. But their mindless devotion to him contradicts the way they actually live.

For example, Russell got physically ill over my dead pheasant photo, but do you think for one second he got sick at the ultra violent movies his best friends make? After all, there's more gun violence in an hour on American movie, television, and computer screens than in the entire United States in a year. I think these movies are awesome because they're just one big gun ad for the NRA after another. You'd think these stars would be the most pro-gun, pro-NRA people in the nation. Instead, they hate the NRA with more fervor than they hate al Qaeda—and frequently compare the two. They advocate for tighter gun restrictions, demand terrorists get out of Gitmo, and walk around with armed bodyguards.

And it never occurs to them that what they're doing on screen might actually contribute to the gun violence they claim to hate. (Oh yeah, I should add that Jamie Foxx's movie *Django Unchained* debuted a month after he called Obama his savior. It somehow managed to have sixty-four grisly deaths in a mere 165 minutes.)

And don't get me started on this "green" trend.

The Hollywood elite have gigantic homes, luxury SUVs, exotic sports cars, and live in thirty-thousand-square-foot mansions with infinity pools. They fly in private jets across the globe— sometimes just for lunch. (Oh, and at Bungalow 8, of course, they might have avoided the paparazzi by taking the helicopter home.)

In other words, their carbon footprint is bigger than Sasquatch's, but they get on social media and try to shame average Americans for doing basic things like heating their homes.

Please.

Have you ever noticed how environmentally disrespectful a typical action movie is? When Will Smith is filmed in car chases and explosions that create pillars of black smoke damaging the ozone layer, do you think he is lecturing the producers about their lack of environmentalism?

Of course he isn't.

What's okay for Obama super-bundler Will is not okay for normal Americans. He can do whatever he wants—and earn tens of millions of dollars doing it—but he's supporting politicians who will shame us into so-called "high efficiency" toilets, driving Priuses, and installing solar panels...which, by the way, no one can afford.

And here's the most hypocritical thing of all. No one even really films in Hollywood anymore. Sure, sitcoms that can be easily made in studios are still produced in California. But dramas—which sometimes cost $3 million per episode—are being filmed anywhere but California.

Why?

Because the taxes are too damn high.

Everything used to be shot there—the enormous state of California offers so many different types of terrain that almost any type of geography could be mimicked well enough to work on screen. But now only 8 percent of filming is done in California, and even the shows set in California are being filmed in

Florida. Why? States have gotten smart and offered tax exemptions and incentive programs to production companies. The production companies have gotten smart and moved their shows to these low-tax states.

As director Michael Corrente said, "Hey, you know what? Studio executives? They'd shoot a movie on Mars if they could get a 25 percent tax break." *USA Today* writer Sharon Silke Carty wrote, "The gypsy-like movie industry…roams from place to place to find the best locations—and best deals."

But wait just a minute. I thought the Hollywood elites don't mind high taxes? Well, they certainly hire the best tax attorneys in the world to make sure they pay as little to the government as possible. And then, when the rubber meets the road, they know what everyday Americans already know: it's better to put money into business than into the bloated federal government's pocket. The bottom line is that they don't mind if *you* pay high taxes. They just don't want to pay them themselves.

But here's the problem. The people I was hanging with at Bungalow 8 are what the culture deems "cool." In fact, they even determine "cool" for the rest of America. No one better epitomizes this than Russell, the godfather of hip-hop. As Jason Mattera pointed out, "the only group powerful enough publicly to resuscitate and resurrect Obama's 2008 mass popularity is the mob of Hollywood Leftists who got him elected the first time."

At Bungalow 8, amongst the "cool" mob of liberal Hollywood elites hell-bent on supporting the Democratic Party, I realized that our nation was in trouble and vowed to do what it takes to fight back.

But not that night. I drained my glass and went back out onto the dance floor. The election was still a month away, and I wanted to have fun during my one night in New York.

THREE

WHY BLACK PEOPLE SHOULD VOTE REPUBLICAN EVERY TIME

*An error does not become a mistake until you
refuse to correct it.*

—John F. Kennedy Jr., quoting Orlando Battista in the *Montreal Gazette*

The hallway was decorated for fall.

Artwork tacked on the walls included scarecrows made from corn, lopsided grins on autumn leaves, and turkeys made out of handprints…little, sweet prints of hands that won't stay small for long. As I meandered to pick up Lola, I realized my night in New York had been just that—a great television appearance, a night with friends that lasted until the wee hours, and way too much Grey Goose vodka and soda with lime. Now, as I walked through the hallways of my daughter's school back in California, I was back in "mommy mode." Normal life.

A black woman came up behind me and grabbed my arm, startling me.

"What are you doing?" I asked.

"Don't worry," she laughed. "You're safe here. We have a secret handshake."

"Okaaaay," I said, though I had no idea what she was talking about.

When she saw the puzzled look on my face, she leaned closer and whispered, "I'm a Republican, too."

If I wanted my party affiliation to be secret, I wouldn't have gone on national television, I thought. I smiled through gritted teeth and yanked free of her grasp.

A secret handshake? Ridiculous.

I went to pick up Lola from class, and she flashed me that bright smile when she saw me. I love that girl. I'd rather spend a lifetime holding her hand and chatting about her days than listening to celebrities self-righteously talk about how they're saving the world by their choice of lightbulbs—before they take off in their helicopters. She grabbed her backpack and ran into my arms.

"How was your day?" I asked.

"I'm going to be in a choir!" she gushed. But before I could hear the whole story, another mom—also black—came up to me.

"I just wanted to congratulate you for speaking out," she said. "I saw you on television, and you did a great job. We *Republicans* need to stick together."

She said the word "Republicans" as if she were coming out of the closet, but only to me. I had no idea she was a conservative, though I'd seen her around the school for months. I got the impression that she didn't want any of her uppity California friends to find out either.

But here's the thing. Our black brothers and sisters fought too hard for equal rights for us to sit back and hide. Or worse, to let white people like Harry Reid, Nancy Pelosi, and Bill Clinton tell us how to think. And certainly our black brothers and sisters fought too hard for equal rights for us to sit back and let black people like Al Sharpton and Jesse Jackson tell us how to vote.

No.

It's time for all black people to get out of the political shackles that have kept us down and to rethink our blind political allegiance to the Democratic Party. In fact, black people should vote Republican every single time. ESPN commentator Stephen A. Smith—who was raised in Queens—spoke about the detriment of the black vote belonging to the Democratic Party:

> Black folks in America are telling one party, "We don't give a damn about you." They're telling the other party, "You've got our vote." Therefore, you have labeled yourself "disenfranchised" because one party knows they've got you under their thumb. The other party knows they'll never get you and nobody comes to address your interest.... I hate the fact that anyone believes that they have a bloc of people in the palm of their hands. That disgusts me. That's never good for America.[1]

He's right, though he only went so far as to say blacks should vote Republican en masse for just one election...to turn over the apple cart, so to speak. That doesn't go far enough, though I confess I had the mentality Smith described—blindly following the Democrats—until the Romney/Obama race.

In 2008, I'd never voted before in my life, but I thought it was time for us to have a black president who could unite us in a profound way. Everyone around me was voting for him, so I cast my virgin vote for a savior who would bring healing and racial harmony. I guess I believed all that shit he shoveled about stopping the oceans' rise and making the world's troubles fade into fairy tales. As it turns out, I was the one believing in fairy tales...that a community organizer could change the world? Did we support him because he was black? Because he looked good on the cover of *GQ* and *Ebony*? Because he gave good speeches?

Obama defended the soaring rhetoric he was fed from his teleprompter in a speech about the power of "just words." He compared his words to those used by great people like Martin Luther King Jr., Thomas Jefferson, and FDR.

But they didn't just give good speeches. They did great things.

Sure Obama is good with words. But in the Bronx where I grew up, what you *do* means more than what you *say*. I've heard plenty of talk from people who want something. Lots of guys have tried that shit on me. I get it. I guess I just didn't expect it from him. I didn't expect this lawyer from Chicago to try to manipulate uninformed black people to vote for him because of the color of his skin. But that's exactly what he did.

When I watched the debates in 2012, I could see it in his eyes—Obama was not being honest, truthful, or transparent. He was always being evasive in his answers. In the Bronx, we call it "talking out the side of your neck." There, if you want me to respect you and listen to what you say, you look me in the eyes or we're not going to talk.

Also, I started noticing how everything suddenly seemed to be about race. How can that be? We elected a black president. Why are we still talking constantly about race? The sad truth I only learned gradually—after I'd pulled the lever for him—was that Obama was using his race to advance his own progressive agenda. He wasn't being honest about what he was trying to accomplish in America. His strategy was obvious—to take advantage of the uninformed to win. I thought Obama had everyone's best interests at heart, especially the best interests of black people. I figured if anyone would know how to lead us to a better place it would be someone who rose from humble beginnings to become the first black president of the United States. It didn't turn out that way, of course. How could he make things worse for all of America—especially for blacks—and yet we kept supporting him?

Even worse, those who *were* opposed to him—like the two black Republican women at Lola's school—were too ashamed or fearful to admit it?

Please.

We've been deceived by race-mongers like Al Sharpton and Jesse Jackson who profit from pretending it's still 1965. We've been fooled into believing that there's still a battle to be fought over race in this country. But here's a newsflash—we won the Civil Rights Movement. We have all the opportunities we could ever need. All we have to do is walk in them. Black, White, Hispanic, Asian—whatever your color and whatever your ethnic background—no one is keeping you down in America but you. Well, you and the Democratic Party that wants to manipulate your vote.

Prior to 2008, black support for the Democratic Party presidential candidate was pretty consistent, between 83 and 90 percent, going back to 1980. But Obama managed to get even more support—95 percent in 2008. Given the historic nature of his candidacy, it's understandable that a record number of blacks turned out to vote. I was one of them. But after four years of seeing how destructive his policies were to minorities, even more of us showed up. I'm ashamed to say that 93 percent of blacks voted for an administration that has only made things worse for race relations in America.

Fool me once? Shame on you. Fool me twice? Well, it's my problem if I choose to stay ignorant.

I was greatly influenced by a YouTube video of *National Review*'s William F. Buckley debating author James Baldwin in 1965 at Cambridge University. Buckley said to Baldwin, "The question...is not whether we should've purchased slaves generations ago, or ought the blacks to have sold us those slaves. The question rather is this: Is there anything in the American dream which intrinsically argues against some kind of deliverance from the system that we all recognize as evil? What shall we do about it?"

In other words, slavery happened. It's time to move on and go beyond what those evil men had in mind when they put shackles on us so long ago. There's no instant cure for our race issues, but we shouldn't throw the baby out with the bathwater. Instead of renouncing the American dream, Buckley said that blacks should address their "own people and urge them to take advantage of those opportunities which do exist and urging us to make those opportunities wider.... If it finally does come to a confrontation between giving up the best features of the American way of life and fighting for them, then we will fight the issue."

Buckley was right. Instead of giving blacks cynicism and despair, we should offer people the tools to succeed, point people to the American dream, and see what enterprising Americans can do.

And we black Americans are enterprising. In the South Bronx, I saw it up close. The hustlers, the pimps, the dealers were doing what it took to avoid the shame of welfare. Yes, shame. Anyone who received government assistance was considered to be lazy and second-rate. They were mocked and teased. Because welfare was so stigmatized, people did other things—usually illegal—to make ends meet. In the logic of the streets, hustling was respected because you were working to make your money. The hustlers lived by a strict code of respect, loyalty, courage, and honor. Plus, it's interesting to note that these hustlers, these pimps, these dealers are natural capitalists.... They make money, they want to keep their money. They're not giving their money away, and Lord help anyone who tries to take it from them—even a dime.

Most black people are Republicans and they don't even know it, because the so-called black leaders on television try to keep them addicted to the tranquilizing drug of liberalism. But every single person is born with an inherent knowledge that what they earn, they should be able to keep. Most black people don't want the government in their business, meddling in things big or small. Most black people believe in a powerful defense. You better believe people in the Bronx sleep with guns under their mattresses and want a government that's also ready and able to defend Americans.

It's time to snap out of it. It's time to wake up.

I think a lot of black people don't want to vote Republican because they believe the lie that Republicans are racists, that Republicans don't like them. That's completely false. Republicans aren't racist. In fact, they really want to get more black support and don't know why they don't. They look at the results of years of liberal policies in big cities, where poverty is still high, and wonder, "Why do you keep voting for the same people?

I wonder the same thing. Why do we keep voting for people who've failed us, who take us for granted? A lot of black people are rightfully upset by what's happening in our cities. Well, who do you think has been running our cities for decades? The Democratic Party. We keep doing the same things in the ballot box, hoping something will change. Isn't one definition of insanity doing the same thing with the hope of different results? Sometimes I feel like the whole pitch of the Democratic Party is something like this: "Your life may be bad now, but if the Republicans get in power, it will be worse."

Well, I want to put that to the test. We've tried your way, and now it's time for a different way. I'm ready to keep more of what I earn, free black kids from failed public schools, and think hard about the right kind of prison reform.

And one more thing—if the Democrats are so comfortable that they've got the right ideas, why do so many of them prefer name-calling to actual debate? I've never experienced as much online abuse as I did when I "came out" as a Republican. Debate my ideas. Your insults just tell me you're weak.

FOUR

THE VOICE NO ONE HEARD

Solitary trees, if they grow at all, grow strong.
—Winston Churchill, quoted in the *Chicago Tribune*

Sometimes people look at me—with my California home and my Manhattan television gig—and think I was born with a silver spoon in my mouth. That my views on politics must have come from a place of privilege. After all, I'm black. How did I get the "white man's" politics? Was I raised by someone who indoctrinated me from an early age—teaching me the ways of William F. Buckley from the womb?

Hardly. In my case, there was a spoon, but it wasn't silver. It was gold and hung around my mother's neck. She wore it like some mothers might wear their children's baby spoons around their necks to remember the first few months of life. I loved the way it lay on her chest, the way it caught the light in certain rooms. Turns out, it was more utilitarian than decorative, because she used it to snort cocaine.

As a child, I didn't know that, of course. I didn't understand the challenges of drug addiction. I didn't know that I came along when my mom was just a teenager. I had no comprehension of the stress my parents must've been under as a couple trying to make it in the Bronx with a new baby. I don't remember exactly when they decided that I was too much for them, but I guess it could've been when I was two. That's when they bundled me up and dropped me off at another family's home in the projects…people, by the way, I'd never seen before. I walked in the door and the house smelled like urine. Above the pungent smell of poverty, the home also had a lingering smell of *sofrito*—a sauté of green peppers, onions, garlic, oregano, and bay leaves that seemed to be the basis of all the food they cooked. The smell permeated everything in the house, lingering even after the meals had been consumed.

"Clean your plate," the mom would say, making sure I finished every crumb before telling me to go play. The father was strict and volatile—he'd give spankings for almost anything—but the mom did her best to take care of my physical needs. She always wore white, because the family practiced Santeria, a voodoo-like mix of Catholicism and superstition. I'm not sure whether my parents knew the family they had left me with practiced Santeria, or whether it would've mattered. But surely they must have noticed that the mom always wore white—like a ghost—and that there was a black *muñeca*, or spirit doll, perched in the kitchen window. The doll, with large creepy eyes, was supposedly protecting the home with her spiritual power. It didn't work. I sensed a bad spirit in that house...something foreboding and dreadful.

"If he calls you to his room don't even think about going." The mom was speaking to me, very sternly, about the family's teenaged son. Her tone scared me, and so did her ominous message, which caused me to keep to myself.

After I had lived with the family for a while, my parents showed up. I breathed a sigh of relief and ran into their arms. I thought I'd be going home, that the past month was a mistake...maybe something came up and they needed a babysitter. An emergency. However, after a quick visit, they took me right back to that house.

"Don't leave me here!" I didn't have the vocabulary to describe why it was so bad. My mom looked at the other mother, whose eyes narrowed a bit. "Oh, go on," she smiled. "She'll be fine."

I scraped at the inside of the closed apartment door, screaming in my despair.

"I want to go home!" Then, I waited, silently hoping that I'd hear my parents on the other side of the door.

"Mommy?" I waited, hearing nothing. "Daddy?"

I could hear the sounds of normal life outside on the street. Kids playing, horns honking, traffic buzzing. But inside, I was trapped in a home that felt unsafe, that smelled of garlic, oregano, and pee. I propped myself up against the door, hoping my parents would return because maybe they would realize they'd forgotten something. Like, for example, me. Eventually, the dad came over with a leather belt and spanked me for crying.

For years, I spent most of my life cooped up, completely dependent on strangers. If I needed to cry, I'd go to the bathroom, sit on the toilet. The walls were peach. Occasionally, my parents would show up with big smiles, but they'd always bring me back when Sunday night came. I did go to preschool, which was a bright spot in an otherwise dreary existence. That's when I began to love education as a way to escape the bad hand I'd been dealt. I'd come home from preschool and watch cartoons. The girls in the family were too old to want to play with me. They were nice enough, but were more interested in boys, clothes, and hair than playing with a toddler.

One night I was playing with an old toy I'd found under a bed.

"Stacey, want some candy?" the brother called from the bedroom next door. I was bored, ignored, alone, and abandoned. If someone offered me candy—someone I saw every day, someone who was a part of what I viewed as my "fake family," someone I trusted as much as anyone else in that house—I was going to take it. For one second, I paused. What was it that the mom had told me? Oh right. I wasn't supposed to go in there. I had obeyed that instruction for a year. In fact, I'd never even seen his room. But what child can turn down candy?

I know. Cliché, right? I wish I could've told you that he pulled off an elaborate trick to entice me to come into his room, but a simple offer of candy caused me to put down the raggedy toy and walk right in. He shut the door behind me. My eyes probably scanned the room to see what sugary treat he had, but found none. I don't remember exactly what happened in his room—this forbidden, off-limits place. But I do remember what happened when I left the room about a half hour later, my tights full of his ejaculate.

I ran my hands through this sticky stuff, but it wouldn't come off. So I came out and walked over to the mom with my hands up in the air. I'm sure I looked like any small child needing help washing up, perhaps before a meal. But when she saw what was on my hands, the mom gasped.

"Why did you do that," she cried. "I told you never to go in his room!" I was filled with shame and regret, though I had no idea what the substance was. I began to cry, as the mom desperately yanked off my tights and ran a rag over me.

I was never the same.

At preschool, I didn't want to be around the rest of the children playing—the children who were so obviously cared for and loved…their moms walking them to school and waving sweetly as their kids disappeared into the school building. Instead, I'd go off by myself and watch the other girls and boys joyfully chasing each other and jumping rope.

The experience of sexual abuse has shaped my life in ways that I can't really calculate. That feeling of "being used" by someone is not easily shaken. Even now, I'm haunted by it. And that deep-seated feeling of dread was exacerbated by a sick story that came out in the news.

When it was reported that outspoken conservative Josh Duggar—the oldest son of the *19 Kids & Counting* family—had molested five girls, everyone was shocked…especially to learn that four of the victims were his sisters and one was a babysitter. Immediately, I felt sick to my stomach. I always do when I hear of abuse. However, it's even worse when outspoken conservatives and advocates of "family values" are involved and don't handle it straightforwardly. (Later, of course, Duggar was exposed during the Ashley Madison hacking, being revealed as someone seeking an extra-marital affair…. This was after he let his family testify to his character and to how he had changed since he was younger.)

The reaction of conservative Christians and Republicans—some of whom seemed to be angrier at the reporting than they were at the abuse—was so distressing that it caused me to momentarily pause and think, "Do I really belong to a group of people who seem so unfazed by molestation? By crimes against children?" Republicans spend a lot of time bellyaching about the way that the liberal media hurts us by mischaracterizing us. In this case, however, we managed to embarrass ourselves without anyone's help.

If Republicans want to be taken seriously, we had better start actually dealing with sex and sexual abuse in a real and meaningful way. Victims of sexual abuse don't want to sit by and watch "celebrity Christians" or famous Republicans minimize sexual crimes. They certainly don't want to see them pouring out an elaborate amount of sympathy for the abusers instead of the abused.

Can God forgive Josh Duggar? Of course. I rely on God's grace as much as or more than anyone. But what Republicans cannot do is mimic the "cheap grace" of modern life…where "celebrities" make public apologies, then are immediately applauded for their "humility." Then, after they establish that they're sorry—really sorry!—they simply go right back to their lives without consequences.

Yes, Mark Sanford, I'm talking to you.

Do you remember that guy? He was governor of South Carolina when he disappeared for four days—the police and even his wife had no idea where he was. His staff said the governor claimed to be hiking the Appalachian Trail during this time, though he wasn't answering his phone and didn't call his family on Father's Day. Turns out, he was with his Argentinian mistress, whom he claimed was his "soul mate." Oops. He had betrayed his wife, his family, and his state, but he still managed to apologize his way to political redemption. He won a congressional seat and then unceremoniously announced on Facebook that he had broken up with his mistress.

By the way, when he was "hiking the Appalachian Trail," he led the Republican Governors Association.

Now I know that Republicans are not the only ones who have had their sex scandals. Of course, I've read all about the Anthony Weiner, Barney Frank, Eliot Spitzer, John Edwards, Kwame Kilpatrick, Bill Clinton, and John F. Kennedy Jr. affairs and cover-ups.

But here's the thing.

Republicans should have a higher standard. We should deal more honestly with our failings. We should hold ourselves to a higher criterion. Conservative voters should demand better.

When we dismiss sexual misconduct—and crimes!—just because the predator was one of "our tribe," it plays into the Democrats' misleading "War on Women" meme, minimizes the pain of the victims, and is just plain wrong.

After all, aren't we the ones who preach about fidelity and family values?

FIVE

THE DECISION MAKER

[This nation was created by people] who are free,
and who mean to remain so.
—Thomas Jefferson

"**L**et's go home."

I lived at that family's house for about three years, until one day my dad showed up and said those three wonderful words.

My *real* home was a walk-up on the fifth floor in the South Bronx. Though I hated walking up five flights of stairs, I didn't complain. I never wanted to be sent away again. When we walked into the house, it smelled of Florida Water, citrus mixed with clove and cinnamon. By now, there was another member of the family: my little brother, who was about four months old. Darien was beautiful—big chocolate eyes and tiny little hands.

I was delighted. I loved holding him and wrapping him in blankets. I was overjoyed at having a family—a real family of my own—to love.

In the matter of one day, my life had changed. I had a mom who dressed stylishly, and who also happened to be drop-dead gorgeous. Plus, I had a slender and handsome father. I'd curl up with him on the couch and watch *The Brady Bunch*. He would hold me so close in his arms, and I'd breathe in the woody, masculine smell of his Aramis cologne.

"Daddy, wake up!" I'd say when he'd invariably nod off while sitting next to me on the couch. "You're missing the best part."

What I didn't understand was that my parents—the people who had rescued me from the family's home—were the same people who had put me there in the first place. I was too young even to read, so I certainly didn't have the ability to process the dynamics of my very dysfunctional family. I guess, in retrospect, it wasn't all that complicated. My parents were druggies.

My mom smoked pot like other people smoke cigarettes. She always had marijuana in her hands, not that she suffered from a lack of versatility. She smoked coolies, which are joints with coke inside. Or, she'd put cocaine in regular cigarettes. Or, to switch it up a bit, she'd sometimes simply freebase. My dad's drug of choice was heroin, which is why he always fell asleep before Jan Brady had a chance to whine, "Marcia, Marcia, Marcia!" Since I was only five, I just figured he was tired from working so hard. Somehow, he had secured a job at Harlem Hospital as a—wait for it—drug rehabilitation expert.

Even though I was not yet old enough to count proper change, my mother used to send me to the store to pick up cigarettes and milk for her. I realized that I was no one's priority.

My mother's brother, Uncle Ferdinand, was the only exception. Even though I was a small kid, he'd take me aside and teach me little life lessons.

Don't be anybody's trick.

Don't settle.

You can do anything you want.

You're special.

Your life doesn't have to be limited to the Bronx.

When the Jesus train comes, make sure you're on it.

Uncle Freddy was always at the house, always looking out for me, and always surrounded by beautiful women. In the neighborhood, he had a certain swagger. Everyone showed him loyalty, honor, and respect. And people who didn't follow that code had to pay the consequences.

When Uncle Freddy and I walked down the street, people on the sidewalk stepped out of the way, made sure they said hello to him, and made sure they shook his hand. When I sat on the front stoop of my building, I'd hear people say, "Don't go over there. That's Freddy's niece." (Later, I can't tell you how many cute boys didn't come talk to me because of my relationship with Uncle Freddy.)

He seemed to be the only person in my life who cared about teaching me how to live. He gave me a vision to see beyond the Bronx, to dream larger dreams, and to never ever let people boss me around. Plus, he was hilarious. "Hey Stacey," he said. "Did

I tell you the one about the parrot who kept getting annoyed his owner offered him a cracker?" Then he'd go into a long joke—more like a story than a joke—and throw his head back laughing at his own profane punch line.

He was really the one who should've been responsible for me. But he wasn't my parent. One night, Uncle Freddy was over at my house, along with my aunts, other uncles, and a few other people. The place was hopping. My dad put a record on, and everyone was smoking, drinking, and laughing. I sat in front of the television in a room adjacent to all of the festivities. Back then, television sets weren't meant to sit unobtrusively above a fireplace or hang discreetly on a wall. Instead, they were big pieces of furniture that took up half the room. There was a little space between the screen and the wood casing that held our television. After a few hours, I'd grown tired of watching cartoons, so I went up to the glass screen and put my hand on it. I'm not sure how, but I got my little pointer finger stuck between the glass and the case.

"Mommy!" I cried out. "Daddy!" I could feel my pulse in my finger. It was so firmly lodged in that small, unforgiving space that I didn't know what to do. "Help!"

But no one heard my small voice above the cacophony of the party. I cried and cried, as loudly as I could, but the laughter and music drowned out my voice. That's when I realized nobody was listening. I was alone. One hour passed, then another. Finally, I decided to stop screaming, simply because I'd run out of energy. It wasn't helping anyway.

Was anyone ever going to come for me?

Then I heard a voice—not *above* the noise of the party, but *instead of* the noise of the party. Though it was different, it was a voice as clear as anyone's I'd ever heard. Immediately, I recognized it as the voice of God.

"It's just you and Me. Pull your finger out."

And so, I took a deep breath and ripped my finger from the television. The skin peeled back and blood began to pour down my hand. I walked into the room where my parents were, and my aunt gasped.

"Linda, come quick!" she said, alerting my mother.

I never told them how long I'd been screaming for them. As my mom hastily washed my hand off and put a bandage on my finger, I looked at all of her friends. They were holding half empty glasses, looking through squinted eyes, laughing at things that were obviously not funny, and stumbling around.

This is it. I thought. *I don't want to be like any single solitary one of you.*

But that incident gave me more than just a determination not to be a partier. It confirmed that I was—in fact—not alone even when it seemed like I was. This was knowledge I would come to rely on, time and time again.

I didn't have the security of knowing where I was going to lay my head at night. Once, my parents took me to my babysitter's house for a nap and didn't return for a week. Another time, they dropped me off with my cousins and didn't come back for a month. And when I was home, things weren't that great anyway. My parents would get into raging arguments that would chill me to the bone.

One morning after a terrible late-night argument—Darien was in his crib, I was watching television, and my teenaged cousins were watching us—my dad told us on his way out the door for work, "Don't wake your mother. She's sleeping."

She was always sleeping.

However, a five-year-old was going to let her mother rest only so long. I was hungry, and I wanted my mother. Sometimes, when my parents were sleeping, I'd wake up, watch cartoons in the dark, and eat cake all day. It was the only food I could find.

After Dad left, I crept into my mother's bedroom and crawled into her bed.

"Mommy," I whispered. "My stomach's growling."

Her eyes were shut, and her mouth was slightly open.

"Mommy!"

She wasn't waking up. I got on top of her and started shaking her.

"Mother!"

When I realized she wasn't waking up, I took my little fingers and pried open her eyes. They were rolled back in her head, so I started screaming.

"Help!" I yelled to my cousins. I couldn't control myself. I didn't know anything about drugs or suicide, but I'd seen death, and I knew I was looking at a shadow of it once again. My cousins ran in and found me screaming while sitting on top of my mom. Next thing I knew, she was being taken away in an ambulance, and Darien and I were sent to my grandparents' house on Long Island.

That was fine by me. They had an acre of land and a teeny house that I saw as a mansion. There was a tall fence behind their house and a sprawling forest—a fun place to explore during the day, but I was always careful to come home before twilight. I had heard the story of Hansel and Gretel, and I didn't want any part of being lost in the woods. My grandmother served us breakfast, lunch, and dinner, which we'd eat at a table...not in front of the television. My grandmother was always singing and tap dancing. She would teach me the steps, and we'd belt out duets. They signed me up for tap dance class, and then came to watch me practice every Saturday. I loved it and was good at it. That's when I really got the dance bug.

Once, during the year that we stayed there, Dad came to visit. I watched him as he put his luggage down in his room. There, in his things, I noticed his bag of drug paraphernalia. I didn't know what the bag contained, but I resented the way the contents seemed to make him act. So I took his gear, climbed the fence behind my grandparents' house, went out into the woods about half a mile, and buried it.

That night, I was sitting on the bed as he unpacked and we chatted about the day. He became increasingly distracted.

"What's wrong," I asked. "Did you lose something?"

Dad dumped the whole bag onto the floor, his hand rifling through socks and tee shirts like he was searching for a grenade that might go off any second.

"No, I'm just unpacking," he said. Then he turned and looked at me. "Did you take something out of here?"

"Like what?" I asked. He must've sensed I was up to something.

"Stacey!" he yelled, grabbing me by my shoulders and shaking me. "Tell me!"

Even though it was already dark, I ran out into the yard, horrified. I'd never seen him like that. I went out to the fence, placed my feet in the slots, and flipped over it. By retracing my steps from that morning and feeling around, I eventually found the place where I had buried his drugs. I still didn't understand what was in this package, but I knew that my dad really needed it.

I returned with the drugs and plopped them on the bed. He grabbed the bag and began digging through it like a man in the desert lunging for water.

—

So, no.

I wasn't born with a silver spoon in my mouth and I wasn't raised being taught Republican principles. I never heard my parents or friends talking about politics, because it was downstream from where we lived. But Margaret Thatcher said it best. "The facts of life are conservative." I think I know what she meant.

When my parents decided to do drugs, there was a consequence for them, for me, for our community.

Consequences. That's something I've tried to teach my kids. Consequences are embedded into the way the world works.

Liberals try to dull them by coming into our communities with programs to help. Whatever problem you have, the government has a mealy-mouthed, ineffective solution.

Let's take a look at what the government has already done, supposedly to help people like me with one of the problems I encountered as a kid: rampant drug use. While I appreciate that the government wants to get people out of that horrible cycle, their well-intentioned program has turned into a quagmire. Over the past forty years, the federal government has spent over $1 trillion on the War on Drugs with almost nothing to show for it. That's $51,000,000,000 per year.[1]

And the social costs are even more staggering. Between 2001 and 2010, 8 million marijuana-related arrests were made. Not only do these arrests cost millions of dollars, they also brand many black kids as criminals forever. A recent study showed that blacks are nearly four times as likely as whites to face arrest for pot-related offenses. I know what you're thinking: black people do and sell more drugs. Not so fast. The study showed that blacks smoke pot at the same rate as their white friends.[2] Fifty-seven percent of those in state prison for drug offenses are black or Latino.

Undoubtedly the "war on drugs" has caused the number of incarcerated Americans to skyrocket.[3] In 2013, there were 2,220,300 people in federal, state, and local prisons and jails. That's one in every ten adults! Did you know America has the highest incarceration rate in the world?[4]

Last, the heavy-handed government show of force in the War on Drugs has done a lot to make America look more and more like a police state.

This is what happens when the government tries to save us from ourselves. I guess we should marvel that it only took them forty years to fail this miserably. Growing up surrounded by drugs and addiction, I didn't have a political bone in my body. Yet I knew from experience that the government wasn't going to help me find a better life. I was the person best positioned to solve my own problems.

The Founders knew this. The Declaration of Independence says we have a right to "life, liberty and the pursuit of happiness." I've always liked that they selected a very accurate word: pursuit.

No one's going to serve it to you on a silver platter. But—in America—you can at least chase happiness. This is the essence of self-governance, which means solving problems as close to the individual as possible. When government bureaucrats start making decisions from their mahogany desks in D.C.—far away from the problems that afflict us—their solutions usually make everything worse. And it's not just Democrats who come up with stupid solutions. (Yes, I'm talking to you, *Mr. Compassionate Conservative No Child Left Behind* George W. Bush.)

Tea Party Patriots founder Mark Meckler said, "America was designed to be a self-governing society, where decisions are made as close to home as possible. Things have changed since Jefferson put down his quill. The government has encroached into every area of life, so infiltrating our culture that we endlessly debate the policies our so-called leaders have decided for us."

He's right. I wonder how Jefferson would feel if he were transported into this nation now and picked up a newspaper.

"Obamacare?" he might ask. "Why did you let this happen? Have you even read the Constitution?"

There's no telling what Jefferson would say about how the IRS isn't even trying to hide the fact that they targeted, intimidated, and bullied Tea Party, Christian, and pro-Israel groups. The federal government—under President Obama's "leadership"—effectively undermined ordinary Americans' ability to speak out on causes they believe in by frightening them about their tax returns and burying them in paperwork during a crucial presidential election. The president hamstrung conservative organizations' ability to organize and to express their opinions about issues that are pressing in on us today.

And I'd hate to see Thomas Jefferson's face when he learned that we have $19 trillion in national debt.

Here's what I have learned. Limited government protects liberty best. The Founders created the "checks and balances" system so that the various government branches don't get so powerful and onerous that they take away our liberty. The federal government isn't supposed to act in areas that aren't authorized in the Constitution. But politicians think they're smarter than our Founders. *Checks and balances?* they think. *That's so old-fashioned.* Consequently, the federal judiciary enthusiastically holds the hand of Congress and the White House as they erode the sovereignty of the fifty states and the American people.

It's up to citizens to take a stand and to seize back the power the bloated federal government has taken from us. It's up to individuals to plant their feet firmly on the ground and reclaim their lives.

Who decides?

According to the Founders and the Constitution, the citizens should make the decisions that affect their lives.

That's why I didn't let my family or my upbringing define my life. Thankfully, I was born in a nation that gave me another option: freedom.

SIX

EDUCATION, THE GREAT INTEGRATOR

Education is the key to unlock the
golden door of freedom.
—George Washington Carver

confess: I'm self-taught.

I've been teaching myself through reading newspapers, *National Review*, and many books like *The Fountainhead*, *The Alchemist*, *Hamlet*, and *The Story of O*. Through my self-teaching, I feel like I'm putting myself through college without having to put up with liberal professors trying to indoctrinate me with the elite nonsense of higher education...lessons they teach that might sound sort of reasonable in the classroom but that would never make sense on the street.

No, I didn't go to a single college, but I made up for that by attending so many elementary schools and high schools. Because my parents moved me around a lot, I went to schools in New York, California, and New Jersey. I went to public schools and private schools. I've lost count of all of the schools I've attended, and the ones I remember I can't always recall the names of. (It doesn't help that New York City schools go by number.) I never went to one school for more than two consecutive years of my life. By the time I was six, my parents were sending me to my third school.

I went to schools in wealthy areas and schools in poor areas. So I speak from experience when I say the American school experience is horrible.

One of the main problems I experienced during my academic years was the strong culture of violence. I can't remember the name of my third school in the Bronx, but I do remember the girl who ruled the playground like some sort of queen.

"TaLonna wants to fight you today after school," my friend told me. It was a sentence that stopped me in my tracks. TaLonna was an enormous black girl—probably twice my size and fat. "What'd I do to her?"

"She said you think you're cute," my friend told me, her eyes wide. According to my classmate, TaLonna had called me the ultimate insult: "high sidity." That simply meant she believed I thought I was better than everyone. That I was special.

"Oh, God," I said, dread filling my stomach.

"What are you going to do?" she asked. "She wants to meet you at the corner after school."

I knew I couldn't turn the challenge down. If I didn't show up, my family would have been disgraced.

"What can I do?" I asked.

My heart raced as I planned my attack and walked to the corner after school. TaLonna could take me out with no problem. Since she had me on size, I had to have her on strategy. When I saw her standing there on the street, I immediately looked around to see what I could use as a tool, a weapon. I wasn't a fighter. Already a crowd had gathered. A nervous energy emanated from the kids, and I could tell they were electrified by the anticipation of seeing a fight. I wasn't going to give them what they wanted—a long-drawn-out scuffle with TaLonna scratching my face like a cat. No, I was going to finish it before she realized it had started. I was going to take her out fast.

My eyes scanned the environment. A plastic bag. Half of a wet cardboard box. Leaves the wind had blown into a crevice so long ago that they'd stopped being individual leaves and were now just a damp, brown mush of old leaves and cigarette butts. Nothing useful.

When my eyes met hers, I took her in. She had a tee shirt on that was about three sizes too small. The fabric pulled tightly over her bulging stomach, showcasing her width, her girth. Her ability to simply sit on me in front of all of these classmates to show who was boss. But she wouldn't simply sit on me. No. She wanted to humiliate me, to bring me down a notch or two. And even though I was six years old, I knew the honor of my family rested squarely on my narrow shoulders. Too bad for her, she'd made a critical mistake.

She was standing, nonchalantly, by a brick wall. Suddenly, my plan was clear. Before she even got to the corner—the predetermined meeting place—I ran up to her, grabbed her, and beat her head against that brick wall.

And that was it. I didn't knock her out, but she was probably dizzy enough that she didn't come at me. She struggled to get up, and I pushed her down.

"Get up again and I'm gonna knock your ass again," I said. The people standing around on the corner realized they had missed the big fight, so they ran over to us to see what had happened. My mother's words of advice floated through my head. *The bigger they are, the harder they fall.*

Turns out, she was right. It was a lesson I'd learn again and again. Word got around.

"Stacey beat TaLonna's ass and you don't really want to fuck with her. She's crazy!" That's how I earned my nickname; suddenly I was known around school as Crazy Stacey. I wasn't thrilled about the nickname, but it helped establish my reputation in the neighborhood as someone to avoid. What TaLonna didn't know—couldn't know—was that she was unevenly matched when she decided to pick on me. Sure, she was big, fat, and strong, but I had a secret advantage.

My life had already been filled with grief that my parents never were around and sadness since no one seemed to care whether I lived or died. But somewhere over the past year— maybe during the first few weeks of kindergarten when many American schoolchildren were learning that *a* was for *a-a-apple*—that deep well of melancholy and anguish had turned into fury. Whoever is angrier usually wins.

In third grade, I smoked a joint my cousin gave me and loved the way it felt. I didn't even know it was illegal. I didn't become a "pothead," but I smoked marijuana whenever it was around. My dad tried to protect me from "hard drugs," or at least he tried to hide his use from me. When I was twelve, I caught a glimpse of the truth. One day I came home from school, opened the bathroom door, and was surprised to see Uncle Freddy and my dad both in the small room. They looked up, horrified, and I saw that my dad had a belt around his arms and my uncle was holding a syringe. I still didn't understand, but I knew, judging from the shock on their faces, that I was seeing something not meant for my eyes.

"Shut the fucking door!" Uncle Freddy yelled.

A shudder went through me. He had never spoken to me that way. He was like a father to me, always speaking words of encouragement. Immediately, I shut the door and stood in the hallway with my hand still on the knob. *What did I just see? What were they doing with a belt and a needle?* I didn't know. But I knew it was not good, and that I was afraid.

The next year, my mom packed our bags and sent us to live with my grandparents on Long Island for a year. That's the way things went with us—for large portions of our lives, we were shuttled off to other places.... Of course, this change wasn't bad. I loved being with my grandparents, being in what felt like a stable family, and going to a new school.

In fact, I had a great teacher named Mr. Ackerman, a very dapper gentleman about 6'4". Like a character out of a storybook, he wore a tweed suit every day, wore a bow tie, smoked a pipe, and had an affected English accent. He told us stories about history and science and how they applied to our real lives. Once he gave a talk on why maps are important, how science relates to nature, and how nature relates to our relationships. He allowed knowledge to encompass our entire lives and being. His passion for teaching gave me passion for learning. That year, I was an honor student and even won the Presidential Award in PE.

When we left Long Island, we were told that we wouldn't be going back to New York. Apparently Mom and Dad had gotten a divorce. In Dad's place was a quiet man we'd never seen before, and Mom told us—without much fanfare—that they were getting married. My new stepfather's name was Cecil Holmes, a tall, handsome black man from Guyana (formerly British Guiana). He was a good Catholic, went to mass every Sunday, and never did a drug in his life. In other words, he was a square compared to my father, and very successful as a record executive. In fact, his record label had KISS and Donna Summer. In 1986, he gave The New Kids on the Block their first contract. He seemed to love my mother, and I could tell he enjoyed having her on his arm.

Suddenly, our family had more wealth and opportunities than we'd ever had. Cecil's job was amazing, but it meant we had to move to California when I was in seventh grade. California was no New York. In my old neighborhood, my friends and I ran into each other naturally in the course of the day. Kids were everywhere—playing stickball in the street, jumping rope, and playing hopscotch. That was not happening in California, where everyone had yards and cars and whole acres to themselves.

Mom immediately enrolled us in the local public school in a residential neighborhood in the San Fernando Valley. It had a pretty playground surrounded by eucalyptus trees and big fields circling the school. Though I was going to miss my friends, maybe it was better than going back to New York, where the schools were so violent. Maybe I'd get along a lot better in this sunny, seemingly optimistic place.

One day I came home and found my mom crying.

"What's wrong," I asked, though I scarcely thought that anything truly was wrong. As an addict, her emotions were always up and down. "Are you okay?"

"They got Uncle Freddy," she said.

"Who did?" I asked. I'd never seen anyone even so much as glance sideways at the man. No one would dare cross him.

"Didn't you hear me," she cried. "The cops. They arrested him."

That word hung in the air between us.

"Arrested?"

Apparently Uncle Freddy—my mentor, my one true fan and advocate—went to jail because he was a pimp. The beautiful women he always had on his arms were not just legions of adoring women. They were prostitutes. *His* prostitutes.

I felt like a ship in a storm when the line holding the anchor snaps. He was the one adult on whom I could lean when times got tough. The one person who represented honor and virtue. Without him, I felt untethered, like I could float away to who-knows-where and no one—not one soul—would care. Later, Uncle Freddy also confessed to killing a sixteen-year-old girl and burying her in the woods behind my grandparents' house. He was put in jail for life, and I never saw him again. I never had a chance to tell him how much I loved him, how much he meant to me, or how much he affected my life. Later, my grandmother told me he had a prison conversion. In fact, his newfound faith was the reason he confessed to the unsolved murder.

I missed him so much after he was taken away, and his words of advice always came to me during times of need. One recommendation would come back to me more than the others: when the Jesus train comes, make sure you're on it.

I think, in a weird way, that this was his way of making sure he was going to be on it too. He died in prison, and I can only hope that he felt the love I had for him during his last days.

—

On the first day of school in my new home in California, several buses pulled up to the school. I watched as black kids poured out of them. *Oh, shit,* I thought. I did the math that quick. *They're coming from somewhere, and it's not here.* Because my neighborhood was predominantly white, the government bused black kids in from South Central Los Angeles. It also bused white kids from my neighborhood to South Central L.A. Of course it was a recipe for disaster. The kids that got bused had to get up at 5:00 in the morning. By the time they arrived at school all they wanted to do was fight and sleep. It was obvious they didn't want to be there. The teachers didn't want them there either. And so my new California school was not a respite from violence, but instead a place embroiled in racial conflict. The bused kids stuck together, and the Valley kids stuck together. Since I was black, the Valley kids assumed I was a bus kid. Since I lived in the Valley, the bus kids wanted nothing to do with me.

"You're from here?" the bus kids laughed, pointing at my lighter skin. My hair didn't conform to their standards, either... as they told me repeatedly. "You're not even black," they'd say. Though I had established myself in New York as "Crazy Stacey," my reputation didn't reach to California. They saw me as "high sidity" too, which meant—of course—that I would scrap every single day.

I didn't like to fight. In New York, violence permeated the school...and perhaps the entire culture of the South Bronx. Turns out, California, absolutely dominated by gangs, was no different. The Crips and the Bloods were the most notorious gangs, and membership in one or the other was mandatory...like a class needed for graduation. The reason was simple. One guy alone at school will certainly get jumped. If this guy has a friend, he'll be less of a target. His friend will have his back. This is an age-old principle. Even the Bible talks about it in Ecclesiastes 4: "Two are better than one.... Though one may be overpowered, two can defend themselves."

Of course the guys in Los Angeles weren't thinking of the Bible when they created their groups. But they figured if two is better than one, four is better than two; ten is better than four; fifty is better than twenty. That's how gangs proliferated, on and on until every single student had to decide.

"Crips or Bloods?" I was asked by a friend named Catherine as she and her twin sister Emily walked with me through the hallways on the way to class. Catherine was in one gang but her sister Emily was in the other, a house divided because Emily's boyfriend was already established in a gang. I didn't know which to choose—there was no "how to select the gang that's right for you" quiz in *Cosmo* that month—so I joined the same gang as Emily based on nothing but the fact that her boyfriend was really a nice guy.

That's what breaks my heart. Gangbangers, drug dealers, and hustlers are all made out to seem like horrible people, when they're just trying to survive. They're just doing what they think is the only thing to do, but they're being lied to: white people don't actually hate them, all white people aren't rich, and you don't have to behave like criminals on television to be cool. I know what it's like to believe you have one option—a gang—and to go along with it. Once I joined, my social life was set. Crips or Bloods. Red or blue.

Of course people don't join gangs by filling out a form and sending in an enrollment fee. To join, people have to prove their loyalty through horrible initiations involving revenge shootings, jail time, and more. Thankfully, they didn't make me go through with any of that. Gang members assimilate into various roles. Some are quick-tempered, while others are chill; some fight, others are on the lookout; some make plans, some execute the strategies. The gangs—thankfully—had already noticed my reputation as a brawler, so they let me in without having to prove myself. They called me "the smart girl."

After I chose my colors, I had to dress differently. I had to start wearing khakis and big white tee shirts and a certain color

rag. The gangs took the fact that they didn't have a lot of money—
and therefore couldn't afford nicer clothing—and turned it into
a badge of honor. A pair of khakis, a tee, and a rag were all that
were required to fit in. In fact, anything else was shameful. You
were in or out, and your clothes were a kind of uniform. The first
morning that I was a gang member, I took one look in the mirror
and laughed. I looked like an inmate at Rikers Island.

But my gang membership didn't protect me from the one-off
fights.

The next month, the biggest girl in the school said she didn't
like the way I talked. She was an ugly black girl named Keisha.
Everybody was scared of her—white kids, black kids, everybody.
When I heard that Keisha didn't like the way I talked and wanted
to fight me, I thought, *Oh great*. But here's the thing. I'm not
going to be bullied or intimidated. If I feel for one second that
someone is going to try to hurt me, I'm going to let you know
real quick that's not how it's gonna go down. I'm not going to
stress out about it every day, I'm going to finish it before they even
know it's begun.

I went to the location where Keisha wanted to fight and
scoped it out—a corridor with lockers lining the walls. I'd
learned in New York that I had to act faster and use an element
of surprise. I knew I had to take her out quick before she saw
me coming. As soon as I saw her, I pushed her up against the
locker and took the locker door and I bashed it into her head.
I kept bashing it into her head until she fell to the ground with
her face bleeding. Then I got on top of her and started pounding
her. I was so sick of people telling me that I wasn't good enough

because I didn't live up to their standards. I guess you could say I fought dirty, but she was big and that was the only chance I had. I think I might have killed her if somebody hadn't pulled me off of her.

I guess you can see that I've never backed down from a fight. My stubborn insistence on standing up to bullies twice my size came from necessity . . . but I have to admit it has helped me in life. Without the constant practice of conjuring that strength at school, I'd never have been able to stand up to the bullies that hide behind computer screens on Twitter, blogs, and Facebook as an adult.

My classmates got the message—don't mess with Stacey—but life didn't get easier. I missed my dad and my friends in New York, and I felt like I was in a war zone at school. I didn't get in trouble for fighting—it's amazing what sort of violence was just left unchecked by the teachers. But I would frequently get in trouble for talking back to them. "Here, do pages 47 and 53," the teacher would say, before slipping off to the teachers' lounge for a smoke. I guess I had been spoiled by the example of Mr. Ackerman back in New York, but I could spot lazy teachers a mile away.

———

"What's wrong with you?" my mother asked me when she noticed I was favoring my hand.

"I broke my finger," I said. It was the last day of school in the eighth grade. I had leaned over the water fountain to get a drink when I felt a hand slip up my shirt. Rather, a hand trying to slip up my shirt. I turned around and hit the guy square in the face. He hit me back, and we ended up having a fight right there in the hall. My finger was throbbing and hurt like hell.

"On what?"

"A boy's nose."

I had told my mother that things were bad at school, but we weren't the type of folks who fled danger or left a place scared. Finally, after an entire year of me getting in fights, she relented.

"Okay, I'll send you to private school," she said. When my mother eventually took me to the heart of downtown Burbank to Providence High School, I could already tell this Catholic school would be a welcome change. As a freshman, I met a girl named Cynthia. We became fast friends, and she's still my best friend today.

But my family never stayed anywhere long.

As you can see, I had many layers of problems during my educational years, most that extended beyond the scope of school. However, since my experiences with school have been so harrowing, I'd like to think I learned a few lessons along the way. Here's what I learned about education:

1. EDUCATION IS NOT POSSIBLE AMIDST A CLIMATE OF VIOLENCE AND INTIMIDATION

No one should ever be physically intimidated or harassed at school. If I hadn't had to fight my way through school, I might know Latin by now! But anti-bullying initiatives have been so politicized, it's hard to actually put your support behind them. Take for example, Lady Gaga's "Born This Way Foundation," whose mission statement said it tries to "foster a more accepting society, where differences are embraced and individuality is celebrated. The Foundation is dedicated to creating a safe community that helps connect young people with the skills and opportunities they need to build a kinder, braver world. We believe that everyone has the right to feel safe, to be empowered and to make a difference in the world. Together, we will move towards acceptance, bravery and love."

Doesn't that sound amazing? When Lady Gaga launched the initiative, she talked about her own experience being bullied and how horrible it was for her. (Believe me, Gaga, I understand!) Soon companies like Office Depot partnered with this anti-bullying initiative, signs popped up in their stores, and "Born This Way" merchandise was created and sold on the aisles of America's stores. The Back-to-School items targeted young kids and advertised Gaga's organization to them.

But the "anti-bullying" organization wasn't really about bullying at all. On the organization's blog, Obama was cited as an example of courage because he was "brave" enough to support gay marriage; another example of courage was a student who came out as a transgender; another example was Chaz Bono for the "courage" to undergo gender transformation. The winning "Born This Way" poster was an image of two guys kissing.

Should gay people get beat up at school?

Never.

But celebrities like Lady Gaga use something that everyone can rally behind—anti-bullying—to camouflage a radically liberal agenda that does the opposite of what they claim. (And by the way, this "courage" word is used too much when it applies to people like Chaz Bono and Caitlyn Jenner for undergoing plastic surgery and hormone treatment because they "accept themselves for who they are." Does that make sense to anyone? If they accept themselves for who they are, why did they have to undergo such radical self-mutilation? It's not "courageous" to have plastic surgery...and using that word in that way does a real disservice to people like our American soldiers who have shown true, selfless bravery.)

Lady Gaga's Born This Way Foundation says it's about "tolerance" and "acceptance," but how accepting do you think it would be of a student who doesn't approve of gay marriage or transgender surgery?

Anti-bullying initiatives are very common in American schools, but parents should be wary of the liberal indoctrination that's behind them. Additionally, parents should be aware of this very sad fact: they don't work. Recently, a study of these anti-bullying programs revealed that students who attended schools that had anti-bullying programs were shockingly more likely to be bullying victims than students who attended schools without them.[1]

Since 70 percent of high school students will deal with bullying at some point,[2] parents need to think soberly about how to protect their children. However, submitting them to liberal indoctrination is not the answer.

2. BIG GOVERNMENT = BAD SCHOOLS

I went to school in three states, and I can tell you that the top-down, government-run education system is failing everywhere. It'd be nice to report that our political leaders took a step back and came up with some innovative solutions. Instead, they just push for more of the same big-government solutions. In 2015, President Obama got in front of the press once again to announce another federal program. The program, supposedly designed to help blacks, was an increase in preschool education. But several studies, including those released by his own administration, have shown no significant impacts in education from such programs. A report even gave the nation a D+ for our early education index.[3] I may not have gone to college, but that doesn't sound like a program that's working very well. Yet Obama wants more of it. President Obama also says he wants to increase reading proficiency and graduation rates for minority students—good goals—yet he opposes the school choice options that are already doing both of those things effectively.

What Obama and the Democrats—and even some Republicans—don't understand is that big government solutions are not the answer. No Child Left Behind is a recent big-government flop, because it forces teachers to prepare students to do well only on a specific standardized test, takes authority out of the hands of local leaders and parents, and taxes us more to do so. Race to the Top, President Obama's $4.3 billion initiative, gave states a payoff for getting out from under the NCLB restrictions and suffered the same problems found in most Washington solutions. Throwing federal funds at the problem doesn't provide an answer for a major reason for low student performance: the culture of poverty and the lack of opportunity inherent in that culture. Common Core was supposed to figure out what students should know and how to best measure student progress toward learning it. The result is yet another top-down, big-government program being forced on parents at the taxpayer's expense.

As education results have declined, big government has grown. Not surprising. The solutions we need are the ones that get government out of the way as much as possible so parents and local leaders can develop real solutions, the kind that produce real results in the real world for our kids.

3. IT'S NOT ABOUT THE MONEY

In *Jerry Maguire*, Cuba Gooding Jr.'s character spoke to his agent over the phone and said four words, over and over.

Show me the money.

But unless you've got a really strong stomach, you don't want to look too closely at where the money in our educational system goes. States have spent more than double the amount on education per student since 1971,[4] but national testing scores for seventeen-year-olds remain unchanged.[5] *No statistical difference between scores for students then and now.*

The United States spends more money per student than any other nation in the world, but it's stuck in the middle on international test assessments.[6]

More money isn't going to fix our nation's schools, and neither is screaming about racial discrimination. That's why I say...

4. STOP SCREAMING. START LEARNING.

In 2013, the Obama administration Justice Department sued
the State of Louisiana, claiming that its school voucher program
was discriminatory.[7] When Governor Bobby Jindal demanded
that the federal government abandon its attack, I stood with him
and called for the big-government bullies to back down. They
understood the power of school choice, because "the program
enable[d] around 8,000 Louisiana students from low-income
families in school districts graded C, D or F to use public money
to attend private schools."[8] I spoke up for those students, not
because I'm against public schools, but because I know what it's
like to be stuck in a failing public education system. I know the
difference it made for me when my family could finally afford
to send me to a private school. Failing schools in Louisiana can
improve over time, but these kids didn't have time to wait.

Here's why: less educated men are finding it increasingly
difficult to stay employed, with an unemployment rate 15 percent higher than for the highly educated[9]; less educated women
are significantly more likely to have children outside of marriage
than those who are highly educated.[10] Not getting a good education perpetuates the breakdown of the family and continues the
cycle of poverty, which traps so many in our nation today. In
Home Economics, Nick Schulz connects the dots with this eye-
opening statement: "While just 6 percent of children born to

college-educated American mothers are born out of wedlock, the percentage for mothers with no more than a high school education is 44 percent."[11]

That's staggering.

5. EDUCATION NEEDS TO BE DE-STIGMATIZED FOR MINORITY COMMUNITIES

We blacks have no shortage of opportunity today, but we have to want to learn. We have to want to improve. We have to want to get an education so we can make something better of ourselves and our families. When Frederick Douglass was asked by whites in 1865 what to do for the freed black man, he responded, "I have had but one answer from the beginning. Do nothing with us!...All I ask is, give [the black man] a chance to stand on his own legs!" Freed slave Booker T. Washington, a founder of Tuskegee Institute and one of the most well-respected black leaders in the history of America, once said, "It is important and right that all privileges of the law be granted to blacks, but it is vastly more important that they be prepared for the exercise of these privileges." Of course, racial discrimination shouldn't be permitted. But that's not the problem facing most blacks when it comes to getting a quality education.

Let me explain with a story.

In the middle of tenth grade my mom moved us back to the east coast, this time to New Jersey, where I went to Paramus High School. This public school had the same culture of violence, and—pretty soon—I was challenged to yet another fight. This time, I had to fight the biggest bully I've ever seen, a big white girl who terrorized the school. Why did she want to fight me?

Because I talked like a white girl.

"You do talk like a white girl," my mom told me when she heard of the fight.

This is a theme that keeps recurring throughout my whole life. I've been told, time and time again, that "because you're black," "you have to" do this, "you have to" do that. Now even my own mother was getting in on the act.

"You sent me to the best school," I said, "Because I took advantage of it, you're criticizing me? How does using correct language have anything to do with the color of anyone's skin?" Members of my own family said I didn't think I was black. They called me Oreo. They said I didn't like black people. Somehow, the fact that I wanted to learn made black people feel I was less black. It was hard to really get an education because I had to worry about who I had to fight at lunchtime. I looked at my mother in disbelief, but she didn't even realize she'd said anything offensive.

"What?" she asked, before flicking her ashes into a tray and blowing her smoke in my face. She didn't get it. There was something about the fact that I loved school that made her question my very ethnicity. My *own mom.*

But apparently, I'm not alone. Fox News commentator Jason L. Riley, editor at the *Wall Street Journal*, identifies a significant problem with this story from his own life:

> I was visiting my older sister shortly after I had begun working at the *Wall Street Journal*, and I was chatting

with her daughter, my niece, who was maybe in the second grade at the time. I was asking her about school, her favorite subjects, that sort of thing, when she stopped me and said, "Uncle Jason, why you talk white?" Then she turned to her little friend who was there and said, "Don't my uncle sound white? Why he tryin' to sound so smart?"...

I couldn't help thinking: Here were two young black girls, seven or eight years old, already linking speech patterns to race and intelligence. They already had a rather sophisticated awareness that, as blacks, white-sounding speech was not only to be avoided in their own speech but mocked in the speech of others.[12]

Jason, himself a black man, tells it like it is: "A big part of the problem is a black subculture that rejects attitudes and behaviors that are conducive to academic success. Black kids read half as many books and watch twice as much television as their white counterparts, for example. In other words, a big part of the problem is a culture that produces little black girls and boys who are already worried about acting and sounding white by the time they are in second grade."[13]

These are the kids we need to reach. These are the kids who need to learn how to succeed. What good does it do to gain access to a better education if we don't want to use it because we're afraid of sounding "white"? Each of us must determine to make the most of the opportunities before us—no matter what anyone else may say to keep us down. We must stand and fight for the better and brighter future our children deserve. We don't have to settle for the bondage of expectations handed down to us because of the color of our skin, even when the pressure comes from our own family. Just because your family didn't respect the value of an education or dissed it as "sounding white" doesn't mean you have to make the same mistake. In fact, it was my psychology teacher in high school who gave me some of the best advice ever: "You are not your family. You are who you choose to be." I decided not to follow everything my family and friends told me I should be or do. I made my own choices when it came to learning and improving myself. And so can you.

You may have been ridiculed for refusing to remain stupid and ignorant. You may have attended a failing school. But that doesn't mean you shouldn't fight for better options for your kids—if the Democrats will stop blocking your freedom to do so.

UNLEASHING THE FREEDOM OF CHOICE

Education is the great integrator. If we can empower every-one with a quality education, we can take our country back from the big-government bullies who prey on ignorance. People of all races who are disenfranchised are dependent on these bullies. By freeing them to learn, we can end this cycle of oppression and inequality.

When it comes to educational equality, this nation is behind almost every other industrialized nation.[14] This mires kids in an endless cycle of failure and poverty, even by fourth grade. By that point, African-American, Hispanic, and low-income students are already two years behind the grade level they're supposed to be at. If they even reach the twelfth grade, they can expect to be four years behind.[15] Poor-quality education leads to less education; less education dooms many young people to the bottom rung of the economic ladder. Americans with doctoral degrees earn on average $1,623 per week with only a 2.2 percent unemployment rate. Americans who have attained nothing more than a high school diploma, however, earn a median income of $651 per week and suffer an unemployment rate of 7.5 percent.[16]

How can all students get a fair shake? The same way we go about getting the best deal on anything—shop for it. By unleashing the freedom of choice in education, we can emancipate children of every race from failing schools. We love the power of choice in every other part of life, don't we? Don't like your cell coverage? Switch carriers. Don't like the produce selection at your local grocery store? Go to the one next door. Find out your auto mechanic is ripping you off? There are plenty of other options out there. We have nearly unlimited choices everywhere else, so why not in education? Why should a parent be forced to send kids to a failing school when other options are out there—better public schools, charter schools, private schools, and innovative online learning and homeschool options?

Across America, the idea of using vouchers to fund private school is catching on. In 2013, more than a quarter of a million students used school vouchers or tax-credit scholarships, and thirteen states created additional tax credits, scholarships, and vouchers for tuition.[17] A 2013 report found that "the benefits provided by existing voucher programs are sometimes large, but are usually more modest in size. This is not surprising since the programs themselves are modest—curtailed by strict limits on the students they can serve, the resources they provide, and the freedom to innovate. Only a universal voucher program could deliver the kind of dramatic improvement our public schools so desperately need."[18] As more families are given the opportunity to use vouchers, the demand will only grow. And the evidence overwhelmingly supports them. School choice improves student outcomes, improves public schools, saves money for taxpayers, moves students from more segregated schools into less segregated schools, and improves civic values and practices.[19] One out of every twenty kids in America is enrolled in one of the ever more popular charter schools. While that's encouraging, many charter schools have waiting lists filled with families desperate to get their kids into better learning environments.

Families must be free not only to choose the best schools, but also to demand the best teachers. But students stuck in bad schools—especially those from minority families in low-income areas—have to suffer as the teacher unions fight to protect bad teachers. In Chicago, a big-government mess if ever there was one, "only 28.5 percent of 11th graders met or exceeded expectations on that state's standardized tests. [And yet,] *Newsweek* reported that only 0.1 percent of teachers were dismissed for performance-related reasons between 2005 and 2008."[20] That's just one tenth of 1 percent of teachers who were replaced in a failing district. Can anyone justify these numbers? Only the teachers unions. They use their members' mandatory dues— billions of dollars—to support political efforts. And 93 percent of those contributions go to—wait for it—the big-government Democrats.[21]

When we take the freedom to choose from parents, we replace it with big-government control. When money is no longer connected to the parents who care most about a student's progress, we remove financial accountability from the equation. How different would schools be if parents were thought of as customers, and the child's learning as the product? A lot of schools would be out of business, that's for sure. Instead we have a monopoly where no one seems to care what parents think or whether or not kids are actually learning anything. Crazy! It's like we're still back in the 1860s and have to fight for our freedom to learn all over again. But it's not 1865—or 1965 either.

It's time to stop acting like we're still in bondage. It's time for parents to throw off the bureaucratic chains and take back control of their children's education. Proclaim your own emancipation from the big-government, top-down education system defended by Democrats and defined by poor planning, poor administration, poor teachers, poor academics, poor classrooms, and poor grades.

It's time to demand something better.

SEVEN

THE POWER OF FAMILY

Family quarrels are bitter things. They don't go according to any rules. They're not like aches or wounds, they're more like splits in the skin that won't heal because there's not enough material.

—F. Scott Fitzgerald

I paced nervously outside the door of the Dance Theatre of Harlem. Auditions were at four o'clock, which meant I had three minutes to prepare myself. After Cecil's job required us to move to California, I had found a great ballet studio where I realized I loved dance. When we moved back to the East Coast, I had had to leave my wonderful California studio and start all over again. The Dance Theatre of Harlem was a very competitive school, but my training in California had prepared me well. I tried to calm myself down, but the clock told me it was time to go. Ready or not.

I walked into the studio with my head held high. Ballet was pure. When I leapt, I felt like I was really leaving the earth—where everything seemed broken and hopeless—and I escaped that pain for just a fleeting moment. There was also a certain romance of being on point.

They gave me a number along with what seemed like a hundred other girls. They would tell us the moves to do—show us a combination, then we'd have to replicate it. As the music played, they'd watch us dance, then point at individual girls and say, "You—get out." Harsh, right? After an hour or so, I realized I was one of the last people standing. At the end of the day, they said, "Congratulations, you made it."

I couldn't believe it!

"Just have your parent sign this form," the instructor said, "and we'll see you on Monday!"

When I rushed into my mom's bedroom, she was sleeping.

"I did it!" I told her, handing her the form and gently nudging her awake. "I got into the Harlem Dance School!"

"You're not going," she mumbled.

"What?" I said.

"There's no way you're gonna go to Harlem every day to dance."

I couldn't believe that she didn't want me to take advantage of this opportunity. Or, more accurately, that she wouldn't let me. I'd taken an acting class in California, until my mom made me stop. Then, I'd refocused my life into my ballet. But what good was all that hard work? Every opportunity I got, Mom snuffed out.

"Quit being a dreamer," she said, before rolling over and going back to her own dreamless sleep.

———

It was my sixteenth birthday, and my godfather was at the house. It wasn't a party for me, but every day was a party for my mother. She was right at the coffee table, forming lines of cocaine with a razor like she'd done a million times before. But then she did something new.

"Here, do you want some?" She looked up at me and smiled.

I looked at her, then the lines. Though I'd been around hard drugs my whole life, I had never done them. But it seemed like my years of hard work at school, in acting class, and ballet had never really mattered. I wasn't any better than they were after all. After living in my family for all these years, I didn't need instructions. I leaned down, held one nostril shut with my finger, and clenched my teeth. I didn't want to blow on the line. I snorted it, pulled back on my forehead above my left eye and inhaled sharply a couple of times. What was happening physically at that moment was that the cocaine was being dispersed in my sinus cavity, absorbing into my system. What was happening emotionally was far more complex.

"Just sit back and relax," my mother laughed. "Let it take hold."

It burned like hell, but I liked it. I really liked it.

After that day I shaved my head, became a punk rocker, and started hanging out in Greenwich Village. There creativity emanated from cafes with the cigarette smoke and the aroma of pastries. When I walked through Washington Square, someone might offer me marijuana, someone else might be playing folk songs, another might be reciting a poem. The people who made culture lived in the Village, collaborating, arguing, inspiring, and catalyzing each other into greatness. Greenwich Village opened my eyes to the possibilities of life and art. Consequently, I didn't see the world as something I couldn't have. I wasn't trapped in the Bronx—not for a second. The words Uncle Freddy said to me so many years ago had never left me: *Don't settle. You can do whatever you want. You aren't limited to here.* Now, I finally began to believe him.

Though I began to do a lot of drugs, there was one thing I wouldn't do: smoke cocaine. I hated the smell. The aroma of it always lingered around my mom, the fog of musty dysfunction. With my newfound drug habit, I stopped going to school unless there were tests…and only for the classes I liked. I would find out assignments, do them at home, and then go for the bare minimum requirements. At this point, I just didn't give a shit about anything. Anger became all-consuming, though it was the quiet kind. I became very withdrawn and didn't talk much. I had very few friends.

One day when I was almost seventeen, I was sitting alone at the school cafeteria when I felt someone staring at me. I was used to the attention, since everyone was talking about how much I'd changed lately.

What'd she do to her hair?

What's gotten into her?

Have you seen Stacey lately?

But this was different. I looked up and saw a blonde, blue-eyed Irish kid looking at me. Our high school had all kinds of different groups. I belonged to the "disco" group, but there were also "punks," "nerds," and "dirtbags." This guy was considered a dirtbag because he rode a motorcycle. He and his brothers used to rebuild old Harleys.

When my eyes met his, it seemed like he could see into my soul. We had a stare down, literally. I looked at him and he looked at me. I might have licked my lips! The next thing I knew he got up—our eyes still transfixed—walked over, and said, "Ay, you want to go out?"

He had me at "Ay."

"Maybe," I said.

"I'm taking you riding after school."

How could I refuse? Pretty soon he was coming by every day after classes to pick me up, and I'd jump on his bike. We were inseparable. I felt like I had finally connected with someone in a real, almost magical way. I felt that Mike "got me." The issues with my family receded into the background whenever we were together, so I made sure we were always together.

One night he came and got me around 10:00. I was wearing high heels like always because I'm so short, and I climbed on the bike and we took off. The next thing I knew, we were driving through the forest.

"Where are we going?"

"If I told you, it wouldn't be a surprise."

It was dark and trees were flying by. I couldn't see anything in front of us.

"Are you out of your mind?" I yelled into his ear, pulling my arms around his chest more closely.

"Just shut your mouth."

Oh, hell no, I thought, but I didn't have time to protest. He parked the bike at the bottom of a hill, grabbed me, and threw me over his shoulder.

"Why are you doing this?" I began to scream. "Where are you taking me?"

He ignored me and steadily climbed the hill, me kicking the whole way. Eventually, he put me down on the ground, put his hands on my shoulders, and turned me around. There, before me was the most beautiful sight I'd ever seen: a lake surrounded by low-hanging trees, the reflection of the moon on the water. Oh, and a sleeping bag right by the lake.

It was the most romantic moment of my life. We made love all night—my first time. In fact, the whole summer was one big romantic adventure. It was just Mike and me. That's all that mattered.

Or so I thought. It's easy for teenagers—even for adults, really—to slip into the idea that a fun romantic relationship will solve all of life's problems. That sex will be the thing that makes things better. I didn't know it at the time, but the very thing that I thought was taking me away from my troubles was actually compounding them. In fact, researchers now say that young adults who engage in casual sexual activity are more likely to be depressed and to seriously consider suicide. Casual sex leads to poor mental health—in both guys and girls.[1] Isn't that a fascinating fact—one that feminists should deal with honestly if they really are about the well-being of women?

Many times, Democrats stigmatize Republicans by saying that all conservatives care about are social issues, the so-called "family values" that rob the fun out of life. Democrats, on the other hand, present themselves as being sexually permissive and helping to defend the poor. This, of course, is exactly opposite to the truth. When Republicans talk about "family values," they are talking about solving cultural problems that disproportionately affect the poor. They are talking about poverty reduction, suicide prevention, and much, much more.

Did you know that marriage is our strongest weapon against poverty? It makes you wonder why Democrats attack it. A decline in marriage drives child poverty through the roof. It also increases welfare dependence. Of course, liberals wring their hands when conservatives start talking about "family values" and "traditional marriage" but it makes sense for the government to do what it can to strengthen marriages. If we ever come across a kid who wants to drop out of high school, we immediately encourage them to stick it out. We should view dropping out of marriage as we do dropping out of high school. It's so important to get and stay married for everyone—especially parents in low-income neighborhoods. Children should arrive on this earth within the bond of marriage with parents who are more economically stable.

Our current administration undermines marriage, and it's time to quit "Murphy Browning" everyone who says that family values and traditional marriage are important. In fact, it's time for Americans—including black Americans from lower-income areas—to realize that the smartest thing they can do to help their kids grow up well in America is to stop having sex outside of marriage. Once they are married, they should stay married…and stop supporting liberal politicians whose policies undermine the very lives they pretend to want to help.

Liberal policies and attitudes harm people in the inner cities. I'm speaking not from a place of strength, not from a pulpit explaining how I did everything right and was rewarded for it. I made mistakes—lots of them. Hopefully you can read my story not with judgment, but with an eye toward helping people like me more easily take responsibility for their lives. I didn't understand any of this when I fell in love with the "dirtbag" with the bike. But I knew from the times that my grandmother took me to Catholic mass that sex outside of the benefits of marriage was not a good idea. Against God's plan. A sin.

Guess what? I didn't care. Having someone to love me, to understand me, and to hold me was too big of a temptation. It's hard to turn down affection and love when at home all you get is contempt and scorn. I sank my life and soul into Mike, until one day we had a fight. It was a rather silly fight, in retrospect, but it was a fight nonetheless. We had been arguing more frequently now. But this time when I knocked on his door, ready to make up, his mother answered with a concerned expression on her face.

"Sweetie, I think you ought to go home and talk to him tomorrow," she said. Her voice was kind, with a tinge of pity.

"Why?" I asked. "What are you talking about?"

Then the door opened a bit more, and I looked in the house. I saw Mike—the love of my life—standing there with another girl.

"I don't want to see you again," he said. I guess the "dirtbag" name was appropriate for more reasons than just his motorcycle.

"Come outside and fight!" I yelled at the girl, who slunk further into the house when she saw the anger in my face. "You better get out here, little girl! I'm not playin' with you! I'm gonna kick your ass!"

Wisely, she didn't come outside. On my way out, I kicked over Mike's bike, but it didn't help me feel one ounce better. There was nothing to say, nothing to do. The one person in my life I loved and adored—the person I'd given myself to—no longer wanted to see me. Like everyone else in my fucking life, he left me.

Alone, again.

That was it. For the next three months, I went dancing at clubs all the time by myself; I slept with guys I don't even remember; I woke up a couple of times in places I didn't even recognize, before slipping out, hailing a cab, and making my way home. Not that home was that much better. Thankfully, my teachers liked me, which meant that somehow I was able to pull off high school graduation. I didn't go to my actual graduation ceremony, though. I called my friend David and said, "Hey, did they call my name?" They had. I took his word for it—they called my name, but I never received that diploma. It didn't matter anyway.

I couldn't imagine any sort of real future for me. It was time to end this.

I went to the medicine cabinet and looked for bottles labeled "drowsy." Plenty of options. I dumped the pills into my hand and washed them down with a large drink of water. I put my hand on my neck when the pills scraped on the way down and smiled at the irony. *I'm literally killing myself, so what does it matter if my throat hurts a little bit?*

I sat at the top of the stairs and looked down over the house. I made peace with God. It was quiet, and I didn't even hear traffic outside. My mom and stepdad wouldn't be home for a while, so there was time. The heater came on, and the glow of the kitchen light at the foot of the stairs made the place—which was so full of pain—seem downright cozy. Darien and I had had some good times in that kitchen. As a part of our chores, we'd dutifully start washing the dishes but would end up laughing, telling stories, and spraying each other with the nozzle from the sink. Our antics always doubled the mess—and our work—but we didn't mind. I loved my brother, and any time spent with him was well worth it. I loved watching him grow into a smart little kid. By the time he was old enough to think, he thought strategically. He was always thinking of ways to make money. He created a business loaning his Speak & Spell, Millennium Falcon, and Atari cartridges out to his friends. I loved watching him develop more into a man. But of course he was only twelve at the time. If I went through with this, I wouldn't really see what the future held for him.

Then it hit me.

Darien.

When would Darien be home? I certainly didn't want him to find me. No kid should have to deal with that. If I died, who'd take care of him?

A sense of dread came over me. Many times in life I'd made a mistake—the kind you can't undo—and felt shame and guilt wash over me. But this sensation of regret was so acute that I lost my breath. I had just swallowed God knows how many pills. What had I done to myself? What had I done to Darien?

I darted up and put my hand on the banister to steady myself, though it hardly seemed necessary. I felt fine. *That's good*, I thought. *The pills aren't even working*. I ran to the kitchen to try to throw up and get some water. I had time. I felt fine. When I heard a knock on the door, I jumped. Who could that be? What horrible timing to show up during someone's suicide attempt! Well, it was just as well. The pills I'd taken must've been old, or simply weak. I was filled with gratitude that they didn't work. When I opened the door and saw my friend Eric, I sighed in relief.

"What's wrong?" he asked.

"Nothing," I said. "Come in."

When we sat at the table and began chatting, everything seemed normal. I could scarcely believe that just a few minutes ago I had thought I was staring death right in the face. Life wasn't necessarily good, but I could handle it. I could stick with it and help Darien make his way in the world. But when I looked back up at Eric, I realized I couldn't quite hear what he was saying. His eyes were as big as saucers. His lips were moving, but his words were muffled, like he was talking underwater.

I thought I heard him say my name.

Then, nothing.

———

"How can you be so selfish?!" My body was tucked under crisp white sheets. Fluorescent lights were above me, but they weren't turned on because the sun was pouring in through the window. Too bright. When I squinted, I could see the silhouette of my mother, hunched over the bed, screaming. "How could you do this to me?"

Another person was in the room. Darien. I heard him crying. Apparently Eric had scooped me up and taken me to the emergency room, saving my life. I wiggled my fingers and my toes. Yep, I was alive, but my survival didn't seem to be welcome news to everyone.

"If you're going to do something," my mother said through clenched teeth. "At least do it right."

"Next time," I managed to say, "I won't fail."

Darien began to cry even more.

"I'm taking you to a mental hospital," she said. "Because you're crazy."

Crazy Stacey. I'd heard that before. But in school the nickname had kept people away and protected me. Coming from the lips of my own mother, it was a vulnerability. It hurt. One of my biggest fears has always been somehow losing control of my mental faculties and being left dependent on others. I spent my first years of life dependent on others, and that didn't work out too well. Threatening to take me to an asylum was probably the only thing my mother could've said that would've gotten my attention. In fact, it horrified me.

True to her word, she didn't take me home after discharge. She drove me to a mental institution in New Jersey, a huge facility with imposing beige walls.

"Mommy, Mommy, please don't do this!" I cried. "I'm going to listen! I'm going to be good! I'm not going to do it again!"

"You're selfish and crazy."

"Please don't do this!" I sobbed. "Don't leave me here."

"Get out," she said as she parked the car.

She took me up to the window to sign me in.

I dragged my feet, crying so hard I could barely speak. "I promise I won't ever do it again! I promise!" She turned to look at me. I'm sure I looked like a mess. Surviving a suicide attempt should've filled me with relief, could've given me a new lease on life. But instead I realized the attempt had made my life even worse. "Mommy? Please?"

"Don't ever do that again," she said, before turning around and taking me home.

Two weeks later, we had a disagreement over whether I should go out. I admit it. It was later than proper girls should probably go out at night, but I was no proper girl. Since my own mother had given me my first line of cocaine, I thought we were beyond the pretense of caring about things like rules and social conventions. We stood there arguing in the kitchen, as we'd done many times before. Then, I saw her grab a knife—the kind that you use to cut large slabs of meat—and a lump formed in my throat.

"Put the knife down," I said slowly. I'd seen this move before. Before she had a chance to do anything, my stepdad intervened. He grabbed her and took the knife from her hands. My mom was furious, so she grabbed a bag of frozen collard greens off the kitchen counter and ran after me with it, trying to beat me.

The collard greens are what did it. Finally, after years of neglect and contempt, seeing my mom chasing me with a bag of frozen collard greens pushed me over the edge. I'd had enough.

I ran upstairs, slammed the door to my bedroom, and went to the window. I placed my fingers on the window and yanked. Years of accumulated paint caused it to stick, but eventually it pulled free. The cold air hit my face and I gasped. I wasn't prepared for the cold, though the ground *was* covered in snow. Using my left hand to brace myself, I crawled out onto the windowsill and looked down. My stomach leapt into my throat. I was on the second floor. Nine feet down? Twelve? I was never good at estimating distances. Not that it mattered. I had no option except to jump. I could no longer stomach life within the walls of that house. That's all there was to it. If jumping cost me what was left of my life, then at least my mom would be satisfied that I "did it right" this time. My bare feet pressed into the wood of the windowsill, and I tried to find a soft spot to land, but couldn't see the ground at this hour.

Did I have to do this? Chill bumps appeared on my arms and seemed to be warning me. This is dangerous. This isn't right. But there was nothing "right" about this situation. My own mother had threatened me with a knife. How dangerous is leaping from the second floor compared to living with a drug addict who apparently wants me dead?

I said a prayer and looked down. In the dark, it all looked the same. *Should I keep my legs up?* I wondered. *What is the best way to fall?* I'd never done this before. Instead of leaping, I lowered myself down and held onto the ledge with my fingertips. Then I dropped into the darkness, and—in spite of myself—a little scream escaped from my lips. The snow rushed by my face, stinging. Before I knew I'd left the ledge, I hit the ground with an excruciating thud.

I checked my arms. They worked. My legs. My left one hurt, but it was still functional. I'd done it!

"Are you okay?" Darien's face appeared above in my window.

"Throw me some shoes and a coat!" I said as I shook off the jolt of the fall.

"What are you doing?"

"Please!" I said. "Just help me. I don't have time to explain, but if you ever do anything for me, do it now."

Dutifully, he left the window and appeared back in a moment. My feet were wet and turning to ice fast.

"Are you gonna be okay?"

"Just toss them!"

He held the items out the window, and they fell right down to me.

"Thank you, Darien," I said, looking up at my brother and seeing flashes of our lives together: sitting in front of the television for hours, laughing at Fred and Wilma; playing stickball in the street; spraying each other with water instead of doing the dishes. When he was little I had tried to shield him from a mother who wouldn't feed us, and I hated leaving him there, but Mom had a different relationship with him. She was less combative, more loving, with Darien. He'd be okay with her in a way that I couldn't.

I took one last look at my brother in the window of my room, and ran off into the woods.

I would never return.

—

I ran through the woods and made my way to the train station. I was crying hysterically, that angry kind of crying that dared anyone to cross me. That driving anger allowed me to run through the woods at that hour without worrying about the danger. When I arrived at the Port Authority—which was filled with hookers, homeless people, and the smell of urine—nobody was about to approach me. Not after what I'd just been through.

I got a train into the city, where I crashed at my godfather's place for a while. His house was full of any sort of drug you'd ever want. He kept a bottle of cocaine with a bullet-shaped nozzle that sat on the coffee table. Anytime I wanted, I could just walk through the living room and take a hit. Drugs were available all the time, and I had no reason to refrain. But after a while, I knew I was wearing out my welcome, so I got my own place. Even though I was only seventeen, I was now officially on my own. I got an apartment on the Upper West Side, got a job as a receptionist at a hair salon in Chelsea, and decided to make a way for myself in this world.

I didn't need anyone's help.

Mom didn't want me to act, so that's naturally what I decided to do. The first job I got was for a hair perm commercial for Jheri Curl. To do the commercial, they actually put a perm in my hair. While I appreciated the truth in advertising, my hair was already curly enough.

"You're really good," the producer of the commercial said to me. "Do you have a theatrical agent?"

"No," I said, trying not to look as pleased as I felt.

"You should go see mine," she said, handing me her agent's business card.

I took the card and slipped it into my purse, vowing to call as soon as I got home.

That commercial made my hair unmanageable, but every time I looked into the mirror and saw that head of hair, I knew: I was a professional actress.

Suddenly, I had a new commercial and a lead on an agent— who signed me right up.

"In fact, I think I might have a role for you," my agent said after just a few weeks.

"Well, I hope the role calls for curly hair," I said, still recovering from the effects of the perm commercial. "Are you going to make me ask what it is?"

"*The Cosby Show*," he said, emphasizing each word like he was laying down a gift at my feet. In a way, he was.

"Seriously?" Every Thursday night I sat in front of my television set at 8:00 to see NBC's lineup of comedies—*The Cosby Show*, *Family Ties*, *Cheers*, and *Night Court*—to distract me from my regular life. I'd never seen a television family like the one portrayed on *The Cosby Show*. Yeah, there were *Good Times* and *The Jeffersons*, but those shows were all about race: J.J. was always "scratchin' and survivin'" in the inner city of Chicago, talking about "black Jesus," and poverty; George and Mr. Willis were always arguing and calling each other racial slurs.

The Cosby Show was so refreshing because it wasn't about race at all. Sure, they showcased the music of Miles Davis, James Brown, Stevie Wonder, Duke Ellington, and Dizzy Gillespie. But rather than making a heavy-handed point that America should listen to "black music," appreciate "black art," or understand "black culture," the Huxtables just showcased the things they loved in the context of normal everyday life. The show was about a family. The family was black, yes. But the episodes could appeal to people of any ethnicity. Judging from its massive success, the show did just that. By the time *The Cosby Show* ended, it had become the biggest sitcom hit on American television in two decades. It was the top television show for four years, pulling in 82 million viewers at its height.

I thanked my agent and hung up the phone. Immediately, I picked it back up again. I wanted to shout into the phone, but the dial tone mocked me. I had absolutely no one with whom to share this moment. I was going to be on the show of America's most beloved family, yet I didn't even have one family member to call.

On audition day, I walked in a room and stood in front of a table of people. A couple of the casting directors read from a paper and asked me to act along with them. I read my lines from the script for the role of "Michelle," Huxtable daughter Denise's friend. As soon as I was finished, I could feel it: I'd nailed my lines. Still, I was thrilled to get the call within an hour. I didn't get a "call back," meaning that I'd have to come read again. I'd actually gotten the part, was going to meet Bill Cosby, and was going to be on the top-rated show in America.

On the first morning of rehearsal, I looked out of my window and spotted the black Town Car they sent into Manhattan to take me to the set. The brownstone featured at the beginning of each Cosby episode is actually in Manhattan—at 10 St. Luke's Place—right there in the Village where I had spent so many of my days. However, the family was supposed to live in Brooklyn Heights. Filming occurred at an old studio on the southern tip of Brooklyn, because Cosby was adamant that he didn't want the show filmed in Hollywood.

I got into the back seat and watched the city go by beyond the glass. We took the Manhattan Bridge over the East River. On my right I had an excellent view of the iconic Brooklyn Bridge, and on my left I could see Midtown receding from view.

You're gonna do this, I told myself as I tried to calm my nerves. *This is gonna happen. This is the first step, so you're not crazy. Everybody tells you that you're a dreamer, that you're not gonna pull this off, and that you can't do it. But that's not true. You're gonna do it. This is happening.* I realized my knee was bouncing nervously and tried to still it.

We drove all the way to Flatbush where what was left of the old Vitagraph studio still stood on what looked like a forgotten block between Locust and Chestnut. Many movies had been filmed at Vitagraph (at one time the world's largest movie production company) since the early 1900s. The place had seen better days.

I met Lisa Bonet first in the stairwell. She was really nice, showed me around, and we became fast friends. Then I met Bill on set. He was dressed casually, and it took me a while to get used to the man whose face was so familiar. I wasn't starstruck—far from it—and he seemed kind and genuinely interested in my life.

"Where do you and your family live?" he asked.

"I live alone," I said, in a clipped way that didn't invite further questioning. He didn't pry, but neither did he stop the conversation.

"Awful young to be living alone," he said.

"My parents are addicts, so I don't really…" I let the sentence trail off.

We were waiting on a new script from the producers, since they had a last-minute change that required a fast re-write of the script. In our episode, Denise asked Dr. Huxtable to see her friend Michelle—me—about a delicate medical issue she wanted to keep from her mom and dad.

The "medical condition" that she wanted to keep under wraps wasn't specified, which left the viewer to assume that it related to pregnancy. That meant my character, who was in high school, was sexually active, and I was playing the "bad girl." Dr. Huxtable determined that my problem was simply a bladder infection. He advised me to take better care of myself, but then wondered if his own kids were keeping secrets from him.

On Monday, the actors, directors, and producers had shared notes during the "table read" of the script—called "Denise's Friend"—and the feedback wasn't positive. The secrecy of teenagers was a great, provocative topic, but it wasn't very funny. Bill suggested adding a "family meeting" to the show, which meant the writers had to quickly work on the script and the stage managers had to rearrange everything.

When we got the revised script on the set, we began going through the lines. I knew from the start. The episode was going to be something special. As we went through the lines, the director made sure the cameras were set up properly. I was prepared, but nervous about the filming that we would be doing at the end of the week in front of a live audience of about three hundred people. I had never performed before an audience or done theater. What would it be like to stand in front of people who would respond to my lines immediately? Would it invigorate me, or make me too nervous to remember what I was saying? I almost over-prepared. I had every line down.

When it came time to film, I checked out the outfit the producers had selected for me for the episode: a seafoam green dress with an interesting collar and a brown leather belt that—somehow—connected to my shoulder. The dress was slouchy, no doubt to cause suspicion in the viewers' minds about my character's, well, character. It was loose enough to keep the pregnancy ruse alive.

On the day of filming, Bill became playful—he constantly interrupted the rehearsals to make me laugh or flub my lines.

He improvised, joked, and questioned me during the rehearsal, so that my nerves completely evaporated. Director Jay Sandrich allowed things to be relaxed because he knew that's how the comedian thrived. Bill was used to doing things live and coming up with lines spontaneously. He didn't want to constantly go over the lines—so taping could be more off the cuff and energetic. Which was great except it was sometimes hard to follow him. Instead of saying the line on the script, he'd say something totally different. That would surprise me so much that I'd screw up my line, and he'd just laugh. Or I'd say the line, and Bill simply wouldn't reply.

In the silence, I'd doubt myself. "Oh, am I supposed to say something else?" I thought it was my fault, because I was the new kid on the block.

"Oh yeah, that's right," he'd say. "I'm supposed to say something now."

He was hilarious. Honestly, I think he was just having fun with the audience while also trying to put me at ease. What should've taken one or two takes frequently took ten. Once I started laughing, it was hard for me to get back into character.

"Bill, please, stop," I finally said.

Once, amidst all the joking, he pulled me aside, lowered his voice, and said, "You're gonna go a long way. You know what you're doing, you're a very smart girl, and you're very professional."

That happened in real life—Bill Cosby to Stacey Dash. But there was one fictional moment in the show that touched me almost as deeply. Dr. Huxtable was talking to Michelle about the fact that she'd waited four weeks to seek medical help.

"I don't know your parents," he said. He was wearing one of his signature sweaters and looked every bit the role of "America's favorite dad." "All I know is that if any of my children got into trouble or had a problem and felt they couldn't come to my wife or me, I'd have a fit."

There I was—on a stage in Brooklyn—hearing loving words from a father who was not mine, who was not even a real person. But those words penetrated my heart.

I loved shooting in front of the audience, it turned out. And they seemed to love the episode, especially the newly added "family conference" that Bill had added at the last minute. It began with Cliff telling the kids that they should always feel comfortable coming to their parents if they're in trouble. Everyone nods, agrees, and moves as if the "family meeting" is over. But Cliff doesn't believe they're taking him seriously enough.

What if you got pregnant, he asks.

Theo quips, "Hey, I know it's not me!"

"Okay," Cliff says. "Let's say it is you!" By this time, the audience is roaring with laughter. "What would you do?"

Theo answers that he'd go to his friend first, because he'd fear his dad would get mad.

"Mad? I'm not going to get mad!" He says this like someone who needs to go to anger management classes, eyes popping. "I'm telling you that I wouldn't get mad...Dogs get *mad*. Humans get *angry*!"

The kids turn the tables on their parents and ask some questions of their own. Sondra asks what would happen if Vanessa had a secret relationship with a seventeen-year-old boy; Theo asks what would happen if he took out his dad's car without permission and damaged it. Then Denise asks a question that really cuts to the heart of the "you can tell us anything" idea.

"Mom, I've got one for you. Remember when I spent the night at Jeanette's house a couple of weeks ago?"

"Yes, I do."

"I didn't spend the night at Jeanette's," she reveals. "I spent it at Tommy Watkins's!"

Clair, without saying a word, looks like she is going to go over to Tommy Watkins's house herself and teach him a thing or two.

"Are you *angry*?" Denise asks. The audience loved it! Turns out she's kidding, just to rile up her parents.

The episode was so funny and touching because it encapsulated the beauty and complications of family life: kids straining for independence, parents trying desperately to protect them. It demonstrated that the family bond remains strong amidst complications. Unbreakable, solid.

Jay Sandrich won an Emmy for this episode. I was so proud of my work on this show—not only because of its popularity, but because of what *The Cosby Show* represented. The Huxtables didn't conform to stereotype, the characters were varied in their personalities and interests, and the show wasn't even about race. I'm so proud to have been a small part in such a historic and culture-changing series.

In 2014 *Black-ish*, a show that was supposed to be "*The Cosby Show* for modern times," debuted. I didn't want to audition for it, but my manager Nathan made me go. He said something about needing to put food on the table. One of the lines in my audition was when a man says to his wife, "Didn't you see *Roots?*"

She says, "Yeah," but he knows she has really never seen the iconic miniseries about slavery.

"You've never seen *Roots* because you're not all black," he says. "You're mixed."

"Yeah, well tell that to my ass and my hair," she replies.

I put down the script and looked at Nathan. "Really?" Why would they do a show about being black that has such ridiculous stereotypes? It's the twenty-first century. Get on with it. Are we supposed to believe that one's blackness is defined by hair, body type, and television miniseries preferences? Please. The producers of this show are only perpetuating stereotypes: all black people must play the same sports, think the same thoughts, live in the same type of neighborhood, eat the same foods, and watch the same television. (By the way, I don't even get why a channel like BET exists. I understand Telemundo. Spanish is a different language. But BET? We don't speak a different language, so we don't need a special channel. Are we missing a chromosome? Is there something different about our DNA? If you had an all white channel I think all hell would break loose.)

After *Black-ish* debuted, it even had an episode where the oldest son joined the Young Republicans at school to impress a girl. His parents were apoplectic. His dad said, "There are certain things in life that are just true. Fact: The Earth revolves around the Sun. Fact: Two times two is four. And fact: Black people aren't Republicans. We just aren't. We vote for Democrats." He added, "Sure, the other side may trot out a token black face every now and again, but the fact of the matter is, being a black Republican is something we just don't do."

The mother also reacted very strongly to the news: "Republican?...No!...We don't do that, Dre! We are compassionate liberals who believe in tolerance, acceptance, open-"

Then the dad interrupted: "Yeah, yeah, yeah, whatever. But we're black, alright? That's all that matters. We're black."

With its heavy-handed reinforcement of cultural stereotypes, *Black-ish* was no *Cosby Show*.

I often think back to how much fun I had on the set with the *Cosby* actors, and even afterward. On the last day of taping, Bill pulled me aside.

"Would you like to come to my house sometime for dinner?" he said. "Camille and I would love to host you."

I couldn't believe it! One of the most famous men in America was asking me to dinner at his house. It actually choked me up a bit. I figured Bill could tell that I didn't have a male figure in my life, that I was adrift. He was well known for asking the child actors on the show how they were doing academically and taking an interest in their success. He was so lovely to show concern for me—even though I was just there for one episode.

A couple of nights later, I jumped in a cab and went to the Cosby townhouse on the East Side.

Camille welcomed me warmly. One of the first things I noticed was the fresh-cut flowers in vases scattered elegantly throughout their home. On the set of *The Cosby Show*, I noticed, there were fresh flowers everywhere as well—delivered even on rehearsal days. I heard that Cosby had asked for real flowers— not fake—even though viewers at home wouldn't be able to tell the difference. (This was before high-definition screens.) He wanted the set to feel like a real home…and, I was beginning to see, *his* real home. I could tell that as soon as Camille showed me around. It was tastefully decorated, with antiques, beloved portraits hanging on the walls, a stunning art collection, and simple yet elegant furniture. It was so welcoming.

After we ate, we moved into the living room.

"Would you like some coffee?" Camille asked.

And then we talked. I wish I could remember the topic of conversation, but I was so enamored with the whole feeling of the place it was hard to pay attention. It was almost as if I'd gone back in time…back to a place when everything seemed hopeful and loving, when Americans had a sense of adventure and wide-eyed optimism. At the Cosby house, I felt like good things were possible, like people were industrious, like education could bring people out of poverty, like life was truly and richly beautiful.

But there was one part of the conversation I'll never forget. "You are responsible for your life. You are responsible," Cosby said to me. Then, he added, "No excuses."

I'm sure whatever else was said was just as encouraging, because the conversation made me feel like I was going in the right direction. There I was, in the middle of Manhattan, talking to this man and woman who'd really made it in America, as the raspy sounds of a saxophone and piano emanated from their stereo and the smell of the delicious dinner we'd just eaten still hung in the air.

But there was something else in the air that night…a feeling with which I was utterly unfamiliar: the warmth of an intact family. When I saw how Bill and Camille acted with each other, it was hard not to stare. I didn't know how well-adjusted married people interacted. I had no idea what it should look like. Even my grandparents—whom I loved, and who seemed more stable than my parents—had issues. My grandfather was a Latin lover and always had other women on the side. My poor Gram, who never drove a car in her life, had no recourse. She must've just looked the other way. So watching the Cosbys interact—playful, smart, affectionate—was like watching a National Geographic special. This is what happily married people look like in their natural habitat. I couldn't look away.

Years later, when I heard Cosby had been accused of drugging women to rape them, I immediately thought *this can't be true.* Cosby represented something amazing—something I never had: a strong father in a loving family. Sure, that was all on television and not real life, but my "real life" intersected with his show at a very challenging time for me. When he and his lovely wife spoke words of encouragement to me, I felt like it set the stage for my career and even my life. I guess that's why I refused to believe the women who kept coming out of the woodwork and why I decided to speak out to say that he had treated me as a gentleman would.

But now? Now, I realize I was wrong. We know that Cosby—America's dad—was just wrong. A predator.

When I think of Cosby now, I think of Uncle Freddy—two men who affected my life in a positive way, but who left wreckage behind them. The evil, terrible, unspeakable acts they did cannot be ignored. I'm not sure why we want to elevate certain people and believe they are better than they are. Maybe for the same reason we hope we're better than we are.

Either way, the Cosby family was just as messed up as my real family...and that strikes me as profoundly sad.

EIGHT

SEARCHING FOR A FAIRY TALE

*I never thought I'd have children; I never thought
I'd be in love, I never thought I'd meet the right person.
Having come from a broken home—you kind of accept
that certain things feel like a fairy tale, and you just
don't look for them.*

—Angelina Jolie

Ladies, here's what I learned the hard way. Don't have an affair with a married man: as the saying goes, what he did *with* you, he will do *to* you.

But I guess none of us ever expects to be the other woman. I imagined my life with a stable husband and two kids, but I had absolutely no blueprint for that kind of life. I'd been taught to do cocaine, not to date well. I'd been taught to party, not to marry well.

When liberals talk about sexual freedom, they don't understand how tightly marriage is bound to economic prosperity. In fact, do you know what the number one indicator of poverty is in America? It's not race, it's not educational level, it's whether or not your parents are still married.

Here are the very painful statistics: In America, the poverty rate for single parents with children in 2009 was 37.1 percent. For married couples with children, it was 6.8 percent. In other words, being raised in a married family reduces a child's chances of poverty by about 82 percent.[1]

I, of course, came from a "broken home," which leads to welfare dependence. No one wants to be on welfare. I'm proud I grew up in the South Bronx, and I'm thankful for the lessons it taught me. After seeing up close the devastation of broken marriages, drugs, and really bad choices (by myself included), I realize that nobody wants to live like that. Nobody wants to be a hustler, pimp, a dealer, or on welfare. Where I came from, if you were on welfare you were a lamb to the slaughter. You were used. You were the drug runner. You were the dope fiend. You were the lazy person. You were talked about. You were teased. Because welfare was so stigmatized, people did other things—usually illegal—to make ends meet.

Hustlers, at least, were respected…even if their activities were not necessarily legal.

The poor want to work for their money, they want healthy marriages, they want children.

But in a world of broken marriages, they lack the ability to actually pull it off.

I made a decision about sex—"family values," if you will—that cost me severely for the rest of my life. After *The Cosby*

Show, I was excited about my career, was a little heady with the prospects of my future, and maybe a bit too confident. When I met a man who was already married, I should've gone on by. But I didn't. I lingered. I flirted. And eventually, I ended up having an affair with a married man name Axel.

He seemed to be created for trouble—tall, dark, and handsome—and it felt like he could undress me by simply lifting his eyebrow. Okay, he wasn't tall. In fact, he was short—maybe 5'10"—and I could tell that he worked out at the gym to get strong so he'd appear bigger than he actually was. In addition to being muscular, he was affectionate, possessive, and tough. He had the swagger. When I was with him, I felt like nothing could happen to me. At first, we kept it quiet—sneaking off together to steal time. Eventually, however, we got more brazen and ended up living together at 81st and York. I did all of this behind my family's back, because I knew they would be furious.

Suddenly, I was the "other woman," but—I told myself—maybe a bit more than just that. Axel had a place with me, after all, and I was sure he'd be leaving his wife soon enough. He had a silky smooth way of talking to me that took me to another place. Everything was wonderful for about four months, but then he started acting suspiciously. He wouldn't come home, and he wouldn't give me any explanation.

"Where were you?" I asked him one morning after he hadn't come home the night before. "What were you doing?" But he was not to be questioned. He slapped the shit out of me and knocked me across the room. I was shocked but stood up and shook off the pain.

"I'm sorry, baby," he said, running over to me. He put his hands on my face, looked into my eyes, and said again, "I'm so sorry."

Gradually, things got worse. When we fought—which happened more and more—he punched me. He was strategic about it, though. He'd hit me on every part of my body other than my face. Sometimes I couldn't walk for weeks, but people couldn't tell I was being beaten.

"I'll never do it again. I love you," he said. "I'll never do it again."

I believed him, until I didn't. By the time I realized that my "new normal" was getting the shit beat out of me by another woman's husband, it was too late. We were no longer having a fling, a romance that could be snuffed out as quickly as it had been ignited. By this time he had become maniacal and obsessed. He considered me just a possession. And who was I to argue? A runaway? A girl whose own parents had given her away to strangers? A girl whose own mom had mocked her failed suicide? A girl whose mentor had been arrested for pimping out prostitutes, one of whom he killed? I didn't feel worthy enough to challenge him.

———

When Axel's wife found out about me, she confronted me in a grocery store. I just told her I was sorry. That's all I could say. I truly was. I was sorry I had thought Axel could protect me. I was sorry I didn't leave the first time he hit me. I was just sorry.

It's hard to imagine how thoroughly I had messed up my life in a mere nineteen years. I told myself that things would change if we could start over somewhere new. "Let's get away from here," I suggested one day to Axel. "Let's go to California so I can work on my career."

"California?" he said.

"Yeah, that's where it's at," I said. " I can pursue my acting, and we can get away from it all."

We decided to make the move, but before we left I heard through the grapevine that my mother was living with her drug dealer and was in bad shape. As much as had happened between us, I still loved her. I wanted the best for her. In fact, I had that same feeling that I did when I once saw her in a fight on the street when I was a little girl. I had an overwhelming desire to help her, to fight for her. Plus at this point my brother was fifteen, still in high school, and I knew no one was taking care of him.

Axel and I did a little investigating and discovered where exactly this drug dealer lived. One afternoon we went to his corner, took a deep breath, and knocked on the door. When the door opened, we came face to face with the dealer. He looked at us from head to toe.

"I'm here for my mom," I said, barging right in. The drug dealer shrugged and went and sat down at the coffee table in front of a big plate of cocaine. While I started going up the stairs, I saw him lean over the plate and begin snorting.

"Axel, stay here and make sure he doesn't move."

"Hello?" I called out. "Mommy?" I heard some noise in a room, so I steeled my nerves and walked through the door. The room was pitch black. All I could hear were the sounds of her muffled crying. I got to her bed and reached out to her. When my hands touched her body, I gasped. She felt like a skeleton.

"Are you okay?" I asked. "Oh my God, where's the light? Turn on the light! Where's the light!?"

I fumbled around in the dark until I found a lamp on the side table. It took all of the courage I could muster to turn on the light. When I clicked on the switch, I saw that her eyes were sunken, her bones were protruding, and she was as thin as I'd ever seen another person. Worse, she had no nose—the cartilage between her nostrils was gone.

I began to cry, but there was no time for that now. "Axel! Axel!! Come up here. We have to take her to the hospital."

"We can't!" he said. "She's hysterical."

So was I. "We have no choice!" I screamed. Axel gently wrapped my mother in a blanket, picked her up, and took her to the hospital. When we got there, the doctor took one look at her and said, "Had you not brought her, she'd be dead."

I convinced my stepfather, who was in denial about her condition, to put her in rehab in Florida for six months. That's all I knew to do. She came out clean, but started using alcohol and drugs almost immediately.

———

Our gamble to move to California paid off. I had my agent send out feelers for movies. Immediately he arranged for me to audition for *Moving*, a film about a man named Arlo who gets a promotion and has to move his family from New Jersey to Idaho.

I auditioned for the role of his daughter.

"This is your first big movie audition," my agent told me, but I didn't need him to remind me of that. I was nervous enough. "Here are your sides."

"A sixteen-year-old?" I asked as I read the description of my character. "But I'm twenty!"

"If you get this role with Richard Pryor, you'll be whatever age they tell you to be," he said. "This is a huge opportunity!"

I went to the audition and got to read my lines with Richard Pryor, the dad character, then Beverly Todd, the mom character. Richard was so much smaller than I had imagined, meek, and quiet. Turns out I had great chemistry with Richard and Beverly; I was thrilled when my agent told me that I'd gotten the role. My character didn't want to leave New Jersey, so she sabotaged the move by messing up the house sale.

I loved filming *Moving* with my co-stars Beverly Todd, Randy Quaid, Dana Carvey, and Rodney Dangerfield. My favorite scene involved a swear jar. In the film, the family was attempting to stop cursing by using a jar that sat in the kitchen. Every time anyone cursed, they had to drop in some coins. When we were at the dinner table, I said a curse word.

"Okay, put a dollar in the swear jar," Beverly scolded.

I took the swear jar, put it on the table, and stuffed all of the money from my pocket into the jar. With that taken care of, I went on a profanity-filled tirade about why I wasn't moving to Boise before storming out of the room.

In the movie, Richard was an ordinary guy who gets pushed beyond his limits by movers, his employers, and crazy neighbors. In reality, however, he was kind, almost shy, and had a super sweet demeanor to him. He had a soft-spokenness to him that made you feel like you should lean in to make sure you weren't missing anything.

One day, he mentioned that he was going to go to the races.

"I love horses! Would you believe my Indian name is *Running Horse*? I'm part Indian." Back then no one said "Native American."

His eyes lit up. "Does that mean you're good at picking horses?"

"We can find out!"

During the days we'd shoot scenes with our wonderful cast. But in the afternoon lulls, Richard and I began sneaking off the set and heading off to the tracks at Santa Anita.

"Win, place, or show?" Richard asked me, standing in the Upper Clubhouse. The man in the window—an older gentleman with bushy eyebrows—smiled patiently. He seemed to know Richard.

"What's that mean?" I asked.

"If you put cash on FoxFace to show," he explained, "you get paid if he's in the top three. If you put it on place, you'll collect if he's in the top two. If you say he'll win, then you only get money if he comes across that line first."

"To win, of course," I said confidently, though the only thing I knew about that horse was that I loved its name. It wasn't my money.

"To win," Richard said to the bookie. He reached into his wallet, got out two hundred-dollar bills, and handed them to the man in the window.

Then he turned to his body guard. "I think she can pick 'em. Did you see him in the paddock? The way he's bucking. He's wild. I like him."

It was 1987 when we were placing bets on horses we knew nothing about. By this time, Pryor had already won an Emmy and five Grammys. Though he'd begun his career by modeling himself on Cosby, Pryor was quite a different man—he took on issues of race and inserted profanity into just about everything. When he hosted *Saturday Night Live*, the worried producers instituted a five-second delay because they had no idea what he'd say. His albums were so provocatively named that people couldn't even refer to them in polite company. But in 1983 he signed a five-year deal with Columbia Pictures that resulted in softer and more mainstream films like *Superman III*, *Brewster's Millions*, and *Moving*. He could act, but he didn't have a very scientific method of selecting horses. If he placed money on a horse and won, he'd laugh. If he lost, he'd laugh even more.

"I'm going to count on you to pick the winners," he said.

Though it was fun to be on set, there was something both calming and invigorating about the tracks—the schedule, the energy, the atmosphere. The horses ran one race every half hour.

There was win-place-show wagering, a daily double, a pick six, and a couple of exactas. It was predictable, and we studied the racing forms and the behavior of the horse between the races. I barely glanced at the stats on the thoroughbreds and just went on the way they bucked in the gate, the colors of the jockey's silks, and just plain ole instinct. We would always come back with a little extra money if I picked the horse. Somehow, I always picked the winners.

My career was beginning to shape up nicely, now that I'd been honored to work with legends such as Cosby and Pryor. Though Cosby at the time seemed like the type of person one would aspire to be, I identified with Richard. He never told me about his life, but I got to hear bits and pieces from his bodyguard–spiritual advisor–physical coach Rashan as we hung out on the set.

Richard was raised in Peoria, Illinois. His mom, a prostitute, left him when he was ten years old, and he was raised by his grandmother, an abusive woman who owned several brothels. As a child, he was sexually molested by a priest; he was expelled from school at the age of fourteen. Somehow he made it in Hollywood, masking the pain of his life with jokes about his life, race, and seven marriages. Rumors abounded about his on-set temper flairs. Just a few years before I met him, he'd set himself on fire while freebasing cocaine. Six years later, he was diagnosed with multiple sclerosis, a disease that attacked his central nervous system. To make it worse, he had multiple heart attacks. In other words, he battled his demons just as my parents were fighting theirs—with varying degrees of success.

I was battling, too.

After every day I spent on the set of *Moving*, I'd go home to Axel. I was starring in a huge movie, but our relationship was a mess. I'd leave the set, go back home, and get the shit kicked out of me. He'd push me, grab me, and hit me…but my face was always camera-ready. A broken nose, after all, would've affected my ability to make a living.

"What happened here?" my makeup artist asked me one morning, looking at a gigantic bruise on my arm.

"I fell," I said.

"Off your bike again?"

I paused, trying to remember the string of lies I'd told. I didn't even have a bike. "No, this time, it was in the shower."

She frowned, grabbing a silver container of concealer. "Well, be careful. We're going to have to cover this one up too."

With deception and makeup, I hid my abuse from most everyone, but Rashan instinctively knew something was up. When Axel came around the set, Rashan suddenly got very protective of me. He'd make Axel feel so uncomfortable that he'd leave, but I had problems a protective friend couldn't solve. Even though my boyfriend beat me, I'd go straight back to him in the evenings, where the abuse would start again. Well, it might or it might not. He hit me just enough for me to understand that he could if I made him angry enough.

The set became a solace for me, a place where I was able to get away from the turmoil at home and become a different person. Plus, the movie turned out well. I loved getting to know Richard Pryor—his spirit, his gentleness, his kindness on set.

But my favorite and most memorable times with him were when we'd go off to see the thoroughbred races during the afternoons and try to win—against all the odds.

———

After *Moving* wrapped, I finally realized that Axel was not going to stop beating me. I needed to get out of there as soon as possible but how could I put bread on the table if I left him? With a laser-like focus, I started trying to get more work so I could afford to live on my own.

In 1988, I was cast for a regular role on a show called *TV 101*, about a divorced photojournalist who goes back to his high school to produce a television news program with the journalism class. I played one of his students (Monique), as did Matt LeBlanc—later famous for his role as Joey on *Friends*.

The role was my first in a television series, and the regular paycheck got me one step closer to leaving Axel. I'd tried before and just hadn't been able to do it, but this time would be different. So I made plans. And I waited. The next time he went out of town, I secretly went and got my own apartment. He'd be furious if he knew what I was up to, so I patiently waited for the right moment, kept everything under wraps, and slipped out while he was gone.

I hadn't planned on someone telling him. But one night when I pulled up in front of my building—a location I thought was secret—he was standing at the entrance.

"I thought you were out of town!" I said.

"I thought we lived together," he said.

He ran toward me, grabbed me, and forced me into his car. When we got to his house, he tossed me into the bedroom.

"That's the last time you try to leave me," he snarled as he threw me on the bed. He opened the chest of drawers, and I scanned the room. It was no use. I knew the place intimately. It was not an apartment, it was a duplex. There was one other occupant of the building, but I could tell from the driveway that the neighbor wasn't home. There was no way out except the door, and no one could hear me no matter what I did.

"You're not going anywhere." He had socks in his hands—just normal, everyday athletic socks—and he wrapped them around my wrists. He tightened them, and I inhaled deeply. "What the fuck are you doing?" I asked as he lifted my arms, shoved me to the top of the bed, and tied my wrists behind my head to the bedpost. I pulled down on my arms, which only tightened the socks around me.

"You can't keep me here!" I screamed.

"You're free to leave," he laughed. "If you can."

I strained against the bed post and felt the full hopelessness of my situation. Axel stood over me, pulled back his fist, and punched me in the stomach. I instinctively tried to block it, but there was no use. There was no slack in the socks, none at all. My wrists stayed tied to the bed, and his fist took my breath right out of me. Now I could barely breathe. I lifted my legs toward my stomach into as much of a fetal position as I could manage. Tears rolled down my face, and—between gasps—I managed to say, "You fucking bastard."

"Here's what you don't understand," he said, a vein on the right side of his face bulging out. "You belong to me." I still couldn't breathe, but there was nothing to say. "If you try and leave me, I'll *kill* you." His voice rose in fury.

"What the hell is going on in there?" I heard a voice outside the door. For a moment, I had a wave of hope. I had thought not one soul could hear me. But when the door opened, I saw Axel's friend Antonio. My heart sank. Antonio was always hanging around, and seemed like a larger Puerto Rican version of Axel. But even though he was much larger and more imposing, I knew he always was subservient, doing absolutely everything that Axel told him to do. No questions asked.

"I didn't know she was here," he mumbled before leaving the room.

Axel turned back to me, unbuckled his belt, and moved over to the side of the bed. "I'll take exactly what I want." And then, to my horror, he proceeded to do just that. It didn't take him long to yank off my boots and jeans. I gasped when he forced himself into me, but I tried not to give him the pleasure of hearing me scream. I looked at the ceiling. The light fixture had two bulbs. One had gone out. A crack in the plaster snaked from the corner. I tried to ignore the tearing I felt as he thrust into me.

When Axel left, he called Antonio into the room to watch me. I convinced him to untie me when I needed to go to the bathroom, and he did let me eat. So I guess it could've been worse, but I saw pure evil in his face.

Nighttime came and went. Then came and went again. I couldn't call in to the set to tell them I wasn't able to come in. If

I was ever going to have even the slightest hope of leaving Axel, I had to do well at work. Acting was the only thing I could rely on to get myself out of his grasp. As I lay there, day after day, I imagined what was going on at the set, wondering if people were calling me a diva. Wondering if they assumed I was sleeping off a hangover and simply couldn't be bothered to come to work or even call.

Axel would come and go. When he arrived, I knew what to expect and braced myself for the assault. I went through various stages during this time—fury, defiance, and depression. After a couple of days of being tied, I tried a different approach. My face softened when I saw him and I managed a smile. It was all I could do, and I figured he could see straight through it. But this was my moment. I was an actress, after all, and this was the most important role of my life: the remorseful, repentant lover.

"Come on, Axel," I said to him when he walked in. "I've been here long enough."

"That's for me to decide."

"You know I won't leave you again," I said, trying not to choke on the words. "I've learned my lesson. I'm sorry."

After a few hours on the third day, I had begged, cajoled, cried, and sobbed enough that he believed me. By the time it was over, I'd almost convinced myself. At least for a moment. When he let me go, I kept up the ruse for a while. I went back to the set and made up an excuse for why I hadn't shown up. My mode of operation had never changed since childhood. Don't complain, don't tell, just handle it. But this time he'd gone too far. I was going to leave, I just had to figure out when.

It wasn't fast enough. Within a few days, I was at the house when he got so mad—I can't remember why—that he threw me up against the wall. A photo fell off the wall and glass shattered everywhere. I screamed, and he threw me back into the wall to shut me up.

"What the hell is going on in there?" A loud knocking on the door brought Axel out of the spell of his fury. It was the downstairs neighbor, who'd heard the commotion and come up to check on us.

Axel opened the door, and the neighbor peered in at me, bruised and crying. "I'm going to call the cops if I hear any more of this!"

After smoothing over the situation with the neighbor, assuring him that all was fine, Axel grabbed me and pulled me all the way into his Jeep. I kicked and screamed, hoping to draw attention. "Shut the fuck up," he yelled at me as he stomped on the gas to speed away from his apartment.

I had no idea where we were going. At a stop sign, I looked up at the road signs, trying to get my bearings, when I noticed a police car was at the intersection. With one fast motion, I lunged in front of Axel and slammed my hand on the horn. Thankfully, it wasn't one of those "Road Runner" horns. It was robust and loud. For one moment, it announced to the world, "Help! There's something wrong here!" But just as quickly as it had begun, it stopped. Axel pushed me away with the back of his right arm. I screamed and banged on the window, hoping to get the attention of the cops.

Just then, I felt a sharp pain in the back of my skull, then another blow that landed with such force that I was pushed into the window of the passenger side of the car. I shut my eyes and started kicking the door and flailing my arms. Another punch landed on my head, and I wondered if I was bleeding. I took off my seatbelt and opened up the car door. We were right in the middle of traffic, so people in other cars started honking at the flung-open door. They couldn't get around us.

Thankfully, the police saw what was going on. When I opened my eyes, I saw flashing blue lights reflected in the Jeep's windows. An officer stood outside Axel's window and shined a light into the car just as Axel's fist hit my head. The cop drew his gun and threw him on the grass. I was so disoriented by the jabs in the head that I felt like I was about to pass out. I was bruised and crying hysterically.

"Put your hands on your head," the officer barked at Axel.

"Do you want to press charges?" he asked me.

"Yes," I said between sobs. I couldn't stop crying.

"Do you have anywhere to go?"

I shook my head.

"We're taking him to jail," the officer said to me quietly, away from Axel's hearing. "Make sure you're gone by the time he's out, because we can't hold him."

I called Garner, one of my fellow cast members, and asked him to come get me. Instead of taking me home, he took me to his home, which was in the middle of nowhere. He let me stay the night, and—for the first time in a long time—I felt safe.

The next morning, my heart raced as I repeatedly looked out from Garner's vehicle for Axel's Jeep. It was a Sahara, so it was brown and green and totally tricked out. But as much as I scanned, I didn't see him. When I finally reached the set, I realized I'd been holding my breath. I exhaled, thanked Garner, and went into my trailer. I knew I'd be safe at work, because that's one thing about Hollywood—they keep television sets as secure as Fort Knox. The set of *TV 101* gave me a safe space to operate and time to think.

As long as my personal drama didn't interfere with my occupational life, I'd have a better chance of getting away from Axel for good. The more jobs I got, the more financially secure I'd be and the less I'd need him. After a few hours of working, I'd sunk myself into my character so much that I'd almost forgotten about my turmoil. The horrendous experiences I had felt, the abuse, the damn socks. It just felt like it was a totally different world— a nightmare, almost, from which I'd awakened.

Garner let me stay at his home for a while, as I looked for my own apartment. If I could just get my own place to stay, I could have my life back. The next day, when I was back at work, I thought I had pulled off an escape. That's when I looked up and saw him. Axel was coming at me, his eyes bloodshot and his teeth clenched.

I had no idea how he got on the lot.

"Don't cause a scene," I said as calmly as I could. I didn't want him to embarrass me, or to earn me a reputation as an actress with too much personal drama. I smiled at my fellow cast mates who were standing around pretending not to watch, but they could tell something was up. When Axel stormed up and grabbed me by my arm, I said. "Let's talk in your Jeep."

I know I shouldn't have gotten in, but I couldn't let him ruin my career by making a huge scene on the set. My work would be what saved me. If I let him ruin that for me, I'd be stuck with him forever. As soon as I got in, he punched me, locked the doors, and drove off…leaving about a dozen of my cast mates standing there, stunned.

"You said you'd stay!" he growled.

"I just needed some time to think," I said, already trying to appease him. At one point in my life, I was a person. A woman. An actress. Someone who happened to fall in love with a man who was charming and romantic, who told me he loved me and couldn't live without me. When he hit me, he changed me. Through no actions of my own, I had become a "battered woman." That's what they called it back then. It sounded so fucking pathetic. I didn't want his actions to define me. And yet, there I was.

It was so hard for me to stop giving him the benefit of the doubt. Surely he wasn't a monster. There was one way out: things had to get better. If things improved, we'd look back on this stage of our lives and say, "We were under a lot of pressure back then," and it would seem like a blur, something vague which we overcame. He made it really easy to fall into this trance. He'd put his arm around me and take me places, proud to have me on his arm. At night, he'd talk gently and tell me I was beautiful. My mother had never—not even once—told me that.

But there was a line, and he had crossed it.

We drove up the Pacific Coast Highway, and I could tell he had no idea where he was going.

"Take me back to work, you can't do this," I said. "People saw you take me. If I don't come back, they're going to call the police."

To my surprise, he listened and took me back to work. Not without a warning. "I'll deal with you later."

When I came back to the set, one of the writers for the show pulled me aside and said, "I don't know what's going on with you, but you have to get away from that guy," he said. "Or he's going to wind up killing you."

The words stung. Not only was I embarrassed, I knew he was right. I'd learned my lesson and knew how to cover my tracks. When I got my own apartment this time, I told no one. It was a studio apartment on the fifth floor of an old 1920s building located on Rossmore in Los Angeles. All I had in it was a large white brass bed. I'd always wanted floral linens, but my mom never let me have them. So I went out, bought the prettiest Laura Ashley linen, and created a lovely place to rest. That's all I needed in my apartment, since life was basically night after night of partying. I had a new set of friends...people from the show...people who didn't know Axel. I even branched out and started dating one of my co-stars. On my twenty-first birthday, I got a butterfly tattoo on my shoulder symbolizing that I—finally and mercifully—was free.

I'd found a place where he couldn't find me.

TV 101 was a big part of my plan. It was a good show while it lasted, but it was on opposite *Matlock*, *Roseanne*, and *Who's the Boss?* It only lasted thirteen episodes. When the show didn't get picked up, I had no money and no other jobs. But I did have a pretty vibrant social life. It had been almost a year since I'd left Axel, and I had been dating other people—it was intoxicating to be with men who were really happy to be with me. I felt happy that I'd established myself in Los Angeles without any help from him. Well, I didn't have any money, but I had managed so far.

One day, I ran into a mutual friend.

"So how is he?" I asked. I still loved Axel, if I have to admit it. Sick, I know. I missed that feeling of being taken care of. I never wanted for anything when he was around.

"Do you want to talk to him?" she asked.

Had I been thinking clearly, I would've responded with an emphatic, "Hell no!" But when she offered to connect us, part of me leapt. I had spent so much of my life with him. He knew me. He knew my family. He'd gone with me to help my mom, he'd been there with me when I was in my darkest moments. Sure, he'd *caused* some of my darkest moments, but that was beside the point. What harm could a conversation do?

We chatted on the phone, and I told him the truth about my situation—that I was struggling to make ends meet.

"Listen," he said. "I don't want it to be that way. I've made some money, and I don't want to know you're struggling. Meet me and I'll take care of it."

I didn't even have enough money to pay my rent the next month. I bit my lip and weighed the consequences. Should I accept anything from that guy? Within the day, I was standing with him at his apartment. He handed me a wad of cash and talked gently to me. I'm not sure what words he said, but being with him reminded me of the good times in New York.

"I've changed," he purred into my ear after we—yes—made love. And I believed him. It was like he cast a spell over me, one of security and, believe it or not, even affection. Suddenly, Axel and I were a couple again. He took me out on dates and wooed me. I felt like he was trying to show me that he was a changed man, that things would be different. After all, it had been a year. Surely he had grown up a bit. Eventually we rented a cute house in Los Angeles. As soon as I unpacked my bags, I took a step back and looked at that adorable house. Finally, I thought. I've got it. A man, a home, and enough money to stop worrying about the landlord. That feeling of domestic tranquility lasted two weeks.

"Are you kidding me?" I asked one morning after he hadn't come home the night before.

Immediately, he started hitting me, and the cycle began, once again.

After he beat me, I realized I'd made a grave mistake. I went to the bathroom and sat on the toilet, holding my ribs. I felt like he'd broken one, but maybe it was just bruised. Worse than the physical pain was the growing sense of dread. What had I done?

Correction: I didn't feel like I'd made a mistake; I felt like I was a mistake…that something fundamental about me as a person had shifted. I'd gone back to my abuser. I had no job. I had no options.

I sunk myself deeper into drugs. Pot, pills, coke.

I no longer recognized myself in the mirror. I had fleeting thoughts about throwing myself in front of a train, and wondered what would happen if I went off a bridge. Would I die on impact with the water, or drown?

Finally, one day, I left. I just walked out of the house, got in a cab, and said, "I've got twenty dollars. Take me as far as you can go away from here."

———

I knew I needed to go, but I wasn't sure where I'd end up. I certainly didn't think I'd end up where I am now—with television appearances, a blog, and over half a million followers on Twitter, where I'm able to share my thoughts on the news of the day. Thankfully, as hard as my personal life has been in the past, it has given me a unique perspective on current events and political issues.

For example, the Ray Rice scandal broke right before the 2014 midterms. As you remember, a video published on TMZ showed the former Ravens running back dragging his fiancée out of an elevator at an Atlantic City casino. People originally speculated that she'd perhaps had too much to drink, but later TMZ published another video showing that Rice's fiancée—now his wife—was not drunk. He had punched her so hard in the elevator that it knocked her out.

Because this was the campaign season, the scandal got political really quick. Democrats doubled down on their "war on women" shtick, insinuating that Republicans condone sexual assault, glass ceilings, and the unfair treatment of women at work. National Republican Senatorial Committee spokeswoman Brook Hougesen responded by saying, "Democrats across the country—mostly men, by the way—have sunk to new lows, exploiting deeply personal issues and crimes, ranging from birth control to sexual assault, domestic violence to discrimination in the workforce for their own political gain."

As a survivor of intimate partner abuse, this infuriates me. You know what else makes me mad? Many of the statistics frequently trotted out by liberals about domestic partner abuse are simply wrong. Have you ever heard that one in five college women will be sexually assaulted? The new mantra of the Left is that "the most dangerous place to be in America for women is a college campus." Newspaper reporters, elected politicians, and even President Obama frequently cite this "fact." Thankfully, it's a hoax.

Two prominent criminologists (Northeastern University's James Alan Fox and Mount Holyoke College's Richard Moran) set the numbers straight: "The estimated 19% sexual assault rate among college women is based on a survey at two large four-year universities, which might not accurately reflect our nation's colleges overall. In addition, the survey had a large non-response rate, with the clear possibility that those who had been victimized were more apt to have completed the questionnaire, resulting in an inflated prevalence figure."[2]

Plus, liberals have changed the definition of "sexual assault." The "1 in 5" hoax is based on such a loose definition that it sometimes even encompasses simply sexual experiences that are later regretted. (Who hasn't regretted a sexual experience?) Fox and Moran say respondents were classified as sexual assault victims if they'd experienced "forced kissing" or had intimate encounters while drunk.

Have you heard that 22 to 35 percent of women who visit emergency rooms are being treated for domestic violence? That's also a hoax. This statistic is one that appears everywhere, including leading textbooks on family violence and law. One book uses this bogus figure to say that on domestic violence the United States is comparable to places like Uganda and Haiti.[3] So where did this number originate? Apparently the Justice Department and the Centers for Disease Control have done studies, but they weren't of all women who visit emergency rooms. (By the way, that number is about 40 million annually.) They were referring only to the women who come to the ER "for violence-related injuries." According to Christina Hoff Sommers, this number is around 550,000. Of this much smaller number, about 37 percent were attacked by intimate partners.[4]

That 203,500 women is 203,500 too many, because no woman deserves to be hit or abused. But can we just be honest about the facts? Approximately one half of 1 percent of all women who go to the ER are being treated for domestic abuse.

One more myth liberals are fond of citing relates to domestic abuse and football. Activists trotted out this claim two decades ago based on research from Old Dominion University: more women get abused on Super Bowl Sunday than any other day.

This was repeated on college campuses, printed in newspapers and academic journals, and discussed around the water coolers of America for years. A couple of autumns ago, *Morning Joe* host Mika Brzezinski said, "You look at Super Bowl Sunday. Super Bowl Sunday has the highest rate of domestic violence. There's something about the game! This is a violent game. And domestic violence on Super Bowl Sunday. We've seen the numbers. Why is that?"

What Brzezinski failed to note was that a *Washington Post* reporter had already dug more deeply into the actual claim and realized—oops!—this too is a lie. Even the Old Dominion researchers cited as evidence of the claim agreed their research was misquoted and misused.[5]

So let's get this straight. Intimate partner abuse is evil and its victims should be treated with respect and care. But it does no one any good to lie about it, to make it seem more prevalent than it is, or to try to lay blame at the feet of one political party.

The problem is too serious to play statistical games with. As a woman who has been through the hell of abuse, I implore America to stop making this a partisan issue.

Let's work together to find real solutions. The real "war on women" is the abuse itself—and the blame, political posturing, and finger pointing that politicians do in order to score points at the polls isn't helping. It's got to stop.

NINE

LIFE AND DEATH

We are never defeated unless we give up on God.
—Ronald Reagan

I paid the driver my $20, got out of the cab, and looked around. I couldn't believe I'd finally gotten the courage to ditch Axel, but it felt good. It felt liberating. It felt scary.

"You look lost," a tall man said to me. He was trailed by a couple of guys who looked amused by me standing there with one suitcase and a confused look on my face.

"You don't know the half of it," I said.

"What can I do to help?"

I didn't answer. Why should I talk to this man on the street? I mean, other than the fact that he was sexy as hell?

"It looks like you might need some coffee," he suggested.

That, I could do. His friends left us and we went to a nearby café. Timothy was a New Yorker—in fact, it turned out he came from the same part of the city as I did and we knew some of the same people. But even more interesting? He was a singer. I'd heard some of his songs on the radio.

We chatted for hours, and then—finally—it was time to go.

"Can I drop you off somewhere?" he asked, laying down some cash on the table. I was relieved when I saw him pay for our food, because I didn't want to admit I had no money to my name. When he saw the blank look on my face, he smiled.

"Wanna come back to my place?"

I did.

This began a love affair that would change my life forever... but not because it lasted.

I moved in with him and tried to forget about Axel. I loved Timothy's music, and it was fun seeing his career take off. He was half Sicilian and half black—he walked around like he was the toughest guy in town. At least it felt that way to me. My newfound luck in love, however, didn't solve everything

"I heard Axel's been asking for you," my friend said to me. "Looking for you," she added, emphasizing the word *looking*.

My heart dropped.

"He's pissed that you disappeared."

"Tell him to go get a punching bag," I said. "It'll be like I never left."

But underneath my bravado, my blood chilled. I delved more deeply into my drug use to dull the fear.

One day I lay on the couch, trying not to vomit. The drugs, depression, and fear had created a horrible nausea.

But then I began calculating. When was my last period? A lump formed in my throat. I couldn't even remember. Definitely more than one month. Could it have been three? Four? I didn't quite keep track.

Don't jump to conclusions, I thought. I got myself off the couch and went straight to my gynecologist, a kind man who really seemed to care about me.

"You are, indeed, pregnant," the doctor said. "Four months, to be precise."

I looked at him, stone-faced.

"I'm pregnant," I said to Timothy that evening. I was bracing myself for his disappointment. To my surprise, he immediately broke into tears, leaned over, and kissed me.

"This is great!" he said, squeezing me. "We're having a baby!"

"You can cancel the celebration," I said.

"Why?" he asked, his eyes wide in disbelief. "We can handle a kid." Plus, he already had a baby from a previous relationship. His son was a little toddler already, and I could tell he adored him.

"Not like this."

"You can't have an abortion," he begged.

If I had this baby, I'd be tied to Timothy in a way that could never be broken. As much as I longed for a family and a "normal life," I'd never actually seen a normal relationship and just assumed this one wouldn't last. Especially since he was a musician who was always on the road. One thing's for sure: I couldn't easily leave while toting a diaper bag.

"Please," he begged.

"It's not up to you," I said.

He wasn't angry with me and seemed to handle me with even more care. *Would a baby actually be a good thing?* And so I decided to wait and think, but the next few weeks didn't instill much confidence. Timothy stopped coming home at the right time and started staying out all night. I lay in bed for a couple of weeks and wondered what I was going to do. After turning it over and over in my head, I realized that I only had one option.

—

Timothy was sitting in the waiting room, his elbows on his knees and his head in his hands.

"Please, please, please don't do this," he sobbed. Tears were falling down his face.

"I'm gonna get this abortion," I said. A mother is supposed to protect her children. So, in a way, this abortion would be my first maternal act. I was protecting my child from an unstable relationship and a drug-using parent (me). I was surprised that Timothy had volunteered to drive me to the clinic, but I realize that he figured he'd use the drive as one last and final opportunity to try to change my mind.

The problem he had was that I was onto his game. He was still cheating on me, with probably several women. No matter how much he begged and pleaded with me during the entire drive, I knew I was alone and I'd always be alone.

"Stacey?" the nurse called my name, and Timothy let out a heave. He grabbed my hand, "Please! I'm begging you."

He was standing next to a wall. When I turned to leave, he slid down to the floor and put his head in his hands and cried like a baby. Then I walked in to get the procedure, facing it all alone. I changed into the little white gown, and a tear fell down my face. Then I began crying. Really crying. When I lay down on the abortion table, the nurse put an IV in my arm and left the room. Probably she wanted to get away from what had become heaving sobs. Because I was already in my second trimester, they would have to put me under to take the baby.

I felt misery to the core of my being. I was sobbing so loudly that I figured the nurses would come in to see what was wrong, to see if the IV had shifted to cause me such pain. But the pain was in my heart, in my soul. That searing pain caused me to do something I'd never done before in my life. I called out to God.

Please, God. You've got to tell me what to do. I don't want a sign, I don't want a feeling, I need you to tell me.

And He did.

"Keep your son."

I heard His voice just as clearly as I'd heard it when I was a toddler with my finger stuck in the television. I recognized the warmth, the tenor, the sobriety of it.

My son? It was a boy?

I reached over and ripped the IV out of my arm, causing blood to spurt everywhere.

"Calm down!" a nurse instructed. "Wait a minute."

"No! No!" I screamed. The fact that I didn't know how much time I had to make my wishes known seized me with horror. What if I suddenly realized I wanted to keep my baby—my son— only to wake up and find out that they'd already taken him? "I'm keeping my baby! Stop! Stop! Stop!"

The nurses ran over to me to put pressure on my arm and clean up the site.

"Okay, calm down," my doctor said. "Let's just take a look and see if everything's okay and then we'll decide."

When he did a sonogram, I heard a faint little heartbeat, and that was it. I was overcome with love for this tiny being. And, yes, it was a boy. Many times, Democratic politicians preach the gospel of abortion as if it's one of the sacred rituals of their party. But the fact that abortion gives a permanent solution to what's really a "temporary problem" (though I don't even think you can accurately call a baby a "problem") is one of the biggest travesties of their party. They claim with a straight face that Republicans wage a "war on women," but they are the ones with policies that literally rip females from limb to limb in the womb...the one place that should be the most protective place on earth. I am so glad that I didn't exercise my so-called "right" to kill the baby inside of me. It would've been the biggest mistake of my life, and I'm not sure how I would've emotionally recovered.

That's one thing liberals don't want to talk about. Abortion causes severe regret in many women, regret that's not easily shaken.

Also, I realize how awful this must've been for Timothy. Many times liberals say that men shouldn't have an opinion on abortion—it's the woman's body, after all. But that's exactly wrong. I didn't make a baby by myself. It takes two, and one of them has to be a man. The fact that I was so callous toward Timothy's feelings about his baby shames me. Abortion is not a "women's issue." It's a human rights issue that affects both sexes. After all, probably about half of the babies killed in abortions in America are boys. Doesn't that give men the right to speak on the issue?

Just because a man can't give birth to a baby doesn't mean he can't powerfully defend a baby. And that's what Timothy did that day. The fact that he was so upset about the abortion really affected me. I would keep the baby.

It didn't mean it was going to be easy.

How am I going to take care of him? My mind reeled. *How am I going to change my life to make it worthy of a child?*

I went out to Timothy, who was still in the waiting room, his face splotchy with frustration and grief.

"I didn't do it."

His eyes grew large and he stood to his feet and grabbed me. This time, he embraced me with such relief I felt he might never let me go. I stood there with his big arms around me and allowed myself to feel his comfort. From that day forward during my pregnancy, I never touched another drug or sipped another drink.

Finally.

A reason to live.

———

"Hello?" I fumbled for the phone. It was dark, and I had no idea who could be calling at that hour. I cleared my throat and tried to push the sleep out of my voice.

"I hope you lose your baby," a woman said, then giggles in the background. Timothy was on tour, and his fans somehow got our number and called. *Were they jealous that he was connected to me? Were they more than just fans? How would they know our personal number?* But when he came home, he dismissed the late-night calls, looked at me with those big eyes, and said, "I'll always be there for you, baby." He talked like he was in one of his romantic songs, which—by the way—had become hits.

"Maybe you should come on tour with me," he said. "It might make you feel better, and I don't want to be separated when you're so close to your due date." I thought it was a brilliant idea. Not only would it show all of the hangers-on that this man had a real life and real family, it would let me spend time with Timothy while he was working. I loved how his career was taking off, and it would be invigorating to see it firsthand.

When I was eight months pregnant, he was invited to perform on a nationally prominent late night show.

"Are you going to help me figure out what to wear?" he asked, smiling. We went shopping together and pulled together a good look for Timothy—a gold hoop earring in one ear, jeans, a black tee shirt, a white leather jacket with red sleeves and an upturned collar. This *was* the early nineties, after all. Even though he was touring, he wanted to take advantage of the television opportunity, so he caught a flight to Los Angeles. I stayed in New York and waited for him to come back the next day. It was weird being in a hotel in what used to be my hometown. I whiled away the day wondering about the baby in my body, daydreaming about Timothy's success, and wondering what next amazing job my agent might bring me. Things were suddenly taking off for us. When it came time for the show, I opened a KitKat from the minibar and turned on the television set.

Timothy walked out onto the stage with the mic in his hand. The backup dancers looked sexy, the disco balls on the set were dazzlingly reflective, and the smoky set looked amazing. When he sang his rendition of his song, the crowd leapt to their feet. The host came out on stage to shake his hand. The host usually did this right before going to a commercial break—it was a way to remind the audience of the name of the singer they had just heard. When the host came out and chatted with Timothy, he asked him many questions...including whether he was single. I laughed. He probably asked him that because the women in the audience went wild for him. Part of being with a talented guy in the entertainment industry is that women everywhere are always throwing themselves at him. I'd have to get used to that now that his star was rising.

"Actually," Timothy responded, "I *am* single."

My mouth went dry. Did he just tell a national audience that he was available? With a pregnant woman in a hotel room three thousand miles away? I threw my shoe at the television and watched it fall on the floor. That wasn't very satisfying. So I picked up a glass table and turned it over. It broke into a thousand shards. I looked around me. Everything that was within my grasp I broke, threw, or destroyed.

I'd be raising this child by myself.

———

There's something about being pregnant that stirs up your emotions toward your family.

As soon as we got back from New York, I picked up the telephone.

"Daddy?" I said into the phone. I could tell that he was not expecting to hear my voice. It had been years. Axel had forbidden me from talking to my dad ever since we'd left New York, and—like an idiot—I'd obeyed him. Now I ached over the fact that he was living so far away. I loved my father so much, and now he was totally alone except for the cold comfort of the drugs that had already taken so much from him. We caught up a bit, but things quickly turned serious.

"Stacey," he said more urgently. "I want you to know I love you, and I'll always love you."

I swallowed hard, trying to keep the emotion down.

"Daddy, I feel the same way," I managed. "I love you and always will."

Those were the last words I got to say to him. Two days later, my mother was in California to help with the baby. Though she had never seemed to care whether I lived or died, she suddenly percolated with affection when she heard that a grandbaby was on his way. When she arrived, I was busy secretly trying to figure out a way to be able to afford to leave Timothy. He was frequently gone on tour, so I began stashing away money in one place he'd never look: the boots in my closet. His success gave me ample time to scheme, to plan, and to make arrangements for the moment when I would take my baby and get out of an unstable situation and away from the pain Timothy's cheating was causing me. Two days after I talked to my father, I was upstairs in my bedroom when I heard a blood-curdling scream coming from downstairs.

"What's wrong?" I yelled, coming down the stairs as quickly as I could with my pregnant body. I saw my mother lying on the floor, clutching the phone. "Tell me! What's wrong?"

"Daddy's dead." My brother Darien, who was seventeen at the time, had come home from school that day to my uncle's apartment on Boston Road in the Bronx. When Darien came into the house he found Dad on the floor. He'd overdosed and died of a heart attack after about twenty-five years of addiction to hard drugs.

I fell to the floor and began to sob.

My mother had always told me how worthless I was, that I was a tramp, that I was stupid, that I was selfish. But Dad would take me everywhere with him—for good errands and bad. I'll never forget the drug purchase gone bad that resulted in the deaths of the sellers just moments before we got out of their house.

I was so thankful that I had called him. When my dad died, a large part of my security (maybe all that remained after Uncle

Freddy's surprise arrest) disappeared with him. I was heartbroken. And the next day, I went into labor.

My mother and Timothy were there at the hospital with me, and my eighteen hours of labor was not easy. When it was all over, I had a bouncing baby boy, just as God had told me. I named him after Austen Heller from *The Fountainhead*, a book that has meant a lot to me throughout my years of reading. As I held him in my arms—his little body melding into mine—I looked at his hands and his tiny little feet. He was perfect, and I cried. This child was everything to me. I had to start making better decisions now that my choices were going to affect this little, innocent baby.

Timothy fell in love with him too. He was good with the baby: he changed diapers and doted on Austin. Seeing him lovingly taking care of our son was so nice. There's just something about a baby that gives hope. It makes the world suddenly seem right. And it was, at least, for a while.

But the joy of the new baby dissipated when everyone left. My mother flew back to New York to help take care of the arrangements for my dad's funeral. Timothy left too, because he needed to go back to the loving embrace of one of his mistresses. In fact, throughout my pregnancy, he'd been dating the same girl. But it worked out well enough. While I was alone with Austin, I had time to plan how to get out of there.

After about four weeks, Timothy started staying out even later and then not coming home at all. During a two-day span when he didn't bother showing up, I remembered my vow to leave.

"How's your girlfriend?" I asked. Austin was sleeping in his bassinet when Timothy meandered in.

"You might be his momma, but you're not mine," he said, pointing to the baby. Something about how he dragged Austin into the argument struck me as particularly cruel.

"I can't do this. I don't want to do this," I said. "If you want to be with this woman, then go be with her."

His face fell and his jaw clenched.

"I choose her," he said and walked out the door.

—

There's nothing like being a single mom with a baby to focus your survival skills. I took the money from my boots and got a small apartment across town from Timothy. It was a one-bedroom place, and I kept Austin in his bassinet near my bed.

Months passed without a word from Timothy, but I managed to get by. One night, I heard a knock on the door, and I figured he'd come to see the baby. *Figures he'd come right after I got him to sleep.* But to my surprise, it wasn't Timothy at all.

"Axel?"

"Surprised to see me?" he said.

Here is the honest-to-God truth. As embarrassing as it is, my initial reaction wasn't to run or to scream or to hit him. My first reaction was a smile. A small part of me was happy to see him, someone from the old neighborhood. Someone who knew my parents and knew where I'd come from.

"How'd you find me?" I asked, but I soon realized this would be no romantic reunion. He wasn't there to catch up or to find out what I'd been doing. When he looked at Austin in the bassinet, he didn't look surprised. It seemed that he wasn't surprised by anything in my life, like he'd kept himself apprised of my situation.

"I told you," he said. "You weren't supposed to leave me."

This is when he started hitting me. I climbed to the middle of the bed. That's where I'd go to try to get away from him—right out of reach, to make it harder for him to get to me. I remembered that he kept a gun on his lower right leg, so I lunged for it. He laughed, pulled a gun from his waistband, and asked, "Is this what you're looking for?"

He dragged me off the bed and drove me to the ground. I tried to get away, but he grabbed my feet as I tried to leave. I ended up on my knees in my oversized closet. That's when I felt the cool metal of the gun pressed against my head.

"If you try to leave," he said, "I'll kill you."

At this point, I felt heat on my skin—fear. I couldn't let him shoot me while my son slept in a bassinet just a few feet away. The world slowed down around me, and all I knew—all I could feel—was that I needed to survive.

"Please, God," I prayed. "Just don't let him kill me or hurt my son."

"Come on, Ax," I said, in as smooth a voice as I could muster. "Put the gun away. The baby's right there."

Somehow I managed to calm him down and get him back to the bed. I knew what was coming and that there was nothing

I could do to stop it. Suddenly, I was more aware of Austin in his crib than I was of the gun pressed into my temple. I didn't want my son to see his mother being raped, I didn't want him to wake up to hear my screams. And so I closed my eyes and shut my mouth.

I heard Axel partially undress, then felt him yank up my nightgown. Both he and I were quiet. I tried not to concentrate on my flesh tearing, but tears rolled down my face. The only sound in the room was my head hitting the backboard with each thrust. During the violent encounter, never once did he take the gun away from my head.

Never once did I make a sound.

The boot money ran out, and I didn't feel safe now that Axel knew exactly where I lived.

How on earth can I afford to move?

My answer came in the form of an audition.

My agent encouraged me to try out for a role opposite comedian Damon Wayans, the *Saturday Night Live* alum who went on to be a member of his brother's comedy show *In Living Color.* Damon wrote the movie *Mo' Money* and starred in it as a con man who tries to get his act together for the sake of his younger brother and for a woman.

I did a screen test for the romantic lead. When I got the role, I was both thrilled and worried. Austin wasn't even one year old yet. Filming was going to occur in Chicago over the course of about three months. My mother kindly offered to watch him, so I laid out specific instructions on what was—and was not—allowed with my baby. My stepfather and brother were living with her too, so I figured that she could handle it. With Axel out to get me, my son might've even been safer without me, but leaving him was the hardest thing I ever had to do. My mother brought Austin to Chicago for his first birthday, and I spent the day in agony over how much I missed him. Though it was a hard few months, it paid off. *Mo' Money* dominated the box office and was the #1 grossing film of the weekend. With the money I earned on *Mo' Money*, I was able to get a new apartment where Austin and I could live with my brother, who was going to the University of Southern California. I finally felt like I was making it in Hollywood, and immediately got another gig.

My next movie was to be shot in a cold, rainy state, but I was game for anything. Well, almost anything. I got there and went to the set and we filmed for a few days until one day the director said, "In this scene, you'll be nude."

"There must be some mistake," I said.

"It's right here in the script," he said.

I immediately contacted my agent.

"These people are under the impression that I'm going to do a nude sex scene," I whispered into the phone.

"Come on, Stacey," he urged. "Be reasonable. This is where the money is."

I hung up the phone and went back to my trailer, absolutely furious. By this time, I had enough success under my belt that I didn't feel like they should be treating me like I didn't have options.

I heard a knock on the door of my trailer, which opened to reveal a sorry-looking producer.

"Listen, about all that back there…." he put his hand on my shoulder. "The lead guy heard about it and wants to talk to you in his room about that scene."

"What's wrong with talking on set?"

"He heard you were upset and he just wanted to talk to you about your concerns."

I hesitantly went to the main celebrity's trailer and knocked on the door. He greeted me wearing nothing but boxers.

"I'm glad you came," he said, ushering me into his dark room.

"It's a nice enough day," I said after I noticed that all of his curtains were drawn. "You should let the sun in."

"Come on," he said, climbing into his bed. "Just get in bed with me. I want to watch a couple of scenes with you to make you more comfortable."

I'd heard of the "casting couch" and how female stars sometimes had to sleep around to get ahead. I was shocked that the producers just expected me to hop into bed with a fellow actor. I'm sure there are other actresses who did. In fact, many of my friends in Hollywood didn't think a thing of it, because the joys of fame and money were enticing enough to make it worth it.

But I wasn't going to sleep with this celeb for a role. I knew that. It just took me a moment to realize what was happening and to collect myself. I went and sat on the foot of his bed, my heart almost beating out of my chest. He put on a movie and began explaining what he wanted to do with me.

I stood up, turned around, and said through gritted teeth, "First of all, I'm not fucking you. Second, I'm not doing the sex scene. Third, I'm not quitting so you're gonna have to fire me."

Then I walked out the door.

One of the best benefits of belonging to the Screen Actors Guild was this: If I quit, I wouldn't get paid. But if they fired me, I'd get paid regardless.

The next thing I knew, every producer came knocking on my door.

"Can I take you to dinner?" one said. "Let's try to clean this mess up."

The expensive meal started out okay—filet, cooked rare—though I knew he was just doing damage control. By the time dessert rolled around, the producer was so drunk I had to drive his car back to the hotel.

"This business is absolutely crazy," I said to myself. The producers replaced me with another actress, but I took the money and went back to my son.

—

I heard a sound at the door, and my blood ran cold.

Axel was still unhappy with my disappearing act. I moved from place to place with Austin, always haunted by the fear that he might show up. When I lived in the Valley with my brother, he found me there. And so I had moved in with a friend. My life was full of anxiety as I lived every day looking over my shoulder, scanning parking lots before I got into my car, and checking (and re-checking) all of the locks before going to sleep.

Sometimes, locks just aren't enough.

I had just put Austin to sleep upstairs and was talking with my friend. We exchanged glances.

"Did you hear that?" I asked.

She nodded, so I crept closer to the door to investigate. Just as I got to the opening to look through the peephole, the door flew open. Axel had kicked it open, completely ripping it off its hinges. The door hit me in the head and caused me to fall onto the ground. Before I knew what was happening, Axel had jumped on top of me and begun punching me.

I started kicking, screaming, and fighting with all of my might.

I went to that place—that crazy place where all I felt was fury and all I could see was red. I'd been living in fear for too long. Years of pent-up fear and resentment surfaced and I felt an anger beyond anything I'd ever felt in my life.

Other than making enough noise to get the attention of hopefully some Good Samaritan neighbors, I had two things on my mind. First, Austin was asleep upstairs on the bed. By this time, he was three years old. He could've easily awakened and come down the stairs to see his mother getting beaten up. I could never forgive myself if he saw something like that.

Second, I had a gun upstairs in a shoebox.

Yes, I'd bought a gun, and I don't want to hear one liberal's criticism about that. Though I was not some sort of gun rights activist—and never would've called myself a Republican at the time—I knew this: I had a child and I was going to protect him.

I don't weigh much and I'll never be a match for probably any guy. I always liked to think that when I was attacked, I'd be some sort of badass who could kick and punch my way out of a bad situation. But that only happens in movies. In a physical struggle, even if I began lifting weights every day, I know I'd lose. I know from experience that I'd lose. And guess what? Having Austin made me realize this cold, hard fact: I was sick of losing.

There's a great quote that comes to mind. "Abe Lincoln may have freed all men, but Sam Colt made them equal."[1] I like to change that a little bit to say, "But Sam Colt made women equal to men, if they know their way around a firearm."

And so I got a gun and learned how to use it.

Or I hoped I knew how to use it.

Somehow I slipped out of Axel's grasp and bolted up the stairs straight to my closet and grabbed the shoebox. I grabbed my revolver, which wasn't loaded, and headed to get the ammo. I could hear my friend downstairs yelling at Axel, trying to get him to leave. She knew exactly what I was doing and really wanted to avoid that scene.

"She called the cops!" I could hear her yelling. "You better leave, because she called the cops!"

He apparently wasn't buying it, and I knew I had a limited amount of time. As I fumbled with the bullets, I heard the distinctive, loud plodding of Axel's shoes coming up the stairs. One. Two. Three. Four. His steps were heavy and deliberate. He wasn't afraid of me.

Yet.

I finally got the gun loaded, headed out of my closet, and came down the stairs. I didn't expect him to be already halfway up the stairs. Suddenly, there we were face to face. He saw the gun. I have no idea what he thought was going to happen. Maybe he thought I'd gotten the gun just to scare him. Maybe he thought I didn't have the guts to pull the trigger. Either way, I could tell by the smirk on his face that he underestimated the fierce protectiveness of a momma. I wasn't going to let my son grow up in fear. Nor was I going to let any harm come to him. There, on the stairs, stood the one man who threatened my life. When he threatened my life, he threatened Austin's.

And so I lifted the gun up to his head and pulled the trigger.

It was a tough shot to make, since he was coming up and I was going down. My depth perception was off, and I was so disoriented by fear and anger that I missed. But by this time, I was committed. I wanted to kill him. I pulled the trigger two more times, missing him each time.

However, he got the message loud and clear. Axel ran down the stairs and out of my house.

By this time, I was hysterical, my clothes were torn, I had a black eye, the door was off the hinges, and Austin was crying upstairs. Immediately, I started to disassemble the gun.

It might seem like an odd reflex, but I wasn't used to being near police. I never saw them when I was growing up in the South Bronx, so I wasn't sure what it would be like if they showed up to your house after something so terrible—so very close to being tragic—had occurred. I was already filling with guilt and shame—*Why had I pulled the trigger? What if the bullet had connected?* I shuddered and tried to concentrate on the task at hand.

"Take this," I said, handing all of the various parts of my .22 to my friend. "Get out of here and take these parts with you. Get rid of them however you can, in different locations."

As silly as it sounds, I'd seen this in a movie—*The Godfather Part II*—and somehow fell into autopilot. I didn't want to deal with the police, who I knew would show up momentarily after my neighbors undoubtedly heard the gunshots. I didn't want anyone to know what I'd done, I didn't want them to ask me questions, I didn't want to fill out paperwork, and I didn't want to go down to the precinct with them to fill out a report.

She took the pieces of the gun. "Where should I hide these parts?"

"Go and throw them off the side of the freeway every two miles," I said, off the top of my head. "Just look for places."

Two cops showed up at my door a few minutes after she left.

"Your neighbors reported gunshots coming from this apartment," the shorter one said as he stepped through the opening where a door used to be. He had kind eyes, as if he'd seen this scene too many times and didn't even have to ask questions to understand exactly what had happened.

"Really? Not from here," I said. "I don't have a gun. There's no gun here."

The cop took a look at the door, at my black eye, then at his partner.

"You know, clearly someone kicked the door off the hinges," he said slowly. "Just so you know, had you killed whoever was trying to get you, it would have been justifiable homicide."

"I don't know what you're talking about," I said. "There's no gun."

Right behind where I was talking to the officers were two bullet holes. *Oh God*, I silently prayed. *Please don't let them look up there.*

"So this door..." his voice trailed off and he examined it. "You just doing some remodeling?"

I began to tell him exactly what had happened that night...more or less. I definitely didn't tell them I'd tried to kill a man. As I talked, slowly and deliberately, I knew—with every minute that passed—that my friend had thrown yet another piece of my .22 off the side of the interstate.

If I hadn't had a gun to defend myself that day when Axel came after me—I don't even want to think about what would have happened.

But our freedom to own guns and use them wisely is under attack from those who don't like or understand guns. Our Constitution guarantees our God-given right "to keep and bear arms." It is a moral right given to us by our Creator to defend ourselves and those we love. The government has no business restricting my ability to protect myself. The reality is that having a gun saved my life—and no big-government bully can take that right from me.

Eric Holder has said his failure to increase gun control was the "single failure" of his time as Attorney General.[2] (I can think of a lot of other *actual* failures on his part.) But it was Obama who said people "cling to guns...as a way to explain their frustrations." Well, trust me—if I had died that day, it would have been a frustrating experience. Having a gun to cling to sure did help.

I use guns for two reasons—to hunt and to defend myself and my family. Hunting drives all of my Hollywood friends crazy. I love going hunting and then casually mentioning it to my friends who recoil at the thought—as they relax on luxurious leather sofas—just to see them get all worked up. The movie producers making films that could be ads for the NRA are the same ones saying we should take away everybody's guns. It would be funny if it didn't put real people at risk.

All of them would be quick to defend their right to free speech—and I would defend their right to make violent movies. But our Second Amendment right to own guns is no less of a fundamental right. I'm only alive today because I had a gun— and I used it.

In my case, my gun was not loaded and the ammunition was stored in a separate place. However, even that's not enough for the Constitution-hating liberals in San Francisco. San Francisco's police code says that no one can keep a handgun in his home unless the handgun is either being carried or "stored in a locked container or disabled with a trigger lock." Of course, as constitutional attorney David French (the husband of my collaborator Nancy French) points out, this effectively makes handguns useless for defense when most break-ins and robberies happen—at night when people are asleep and would need to wake up and react in seconds. If San Franciscans are caught breaking this law, they can spend up to six months in jail or be fined up to $1,000.[3]

But if my gun had been locked in a safe or disabled with a trigger lock when Axel showed up, I wouldn't have been able to get to it. When someone is trying to attack you, seconds matter. I know beyond a shadow of a doubt that a gun-carrying woman is less of a target and more empowered than one cowering on the floor waiting for "what's coming to her."

I've been both.

But this time, I chose to be empowered.

I never had to deal with Axel again.

TEN

NOT REALLY CLUELESS

A dream is a wish your heart makes.
—from *Cinderella*

"**G**od, grant me the serenity to accept the things I cannot change, the courage to change the things I can, and the wisdom to know the difference," the man in the front of the room said. A couple of the people bowed their heads, one said, "Amen," and I joined the remaining dozen or so who just looked ahead silently.

It was my first time in Alcoholics Anonymous, and I reached over and squeezed the hand of the blond-headed man to my right. He looked at me with his green eyes and smiled.

"You can do it," Matthew said. He'd been sober five years, which, honestly, was one of the first things that attracted me to him. As I got to know him, I appreciated his laid-back approach to life, his even-temperedness, and his kindness. He was an aspiring actor and already knew me from my past work. His sobriety inspired me to give up drugs as well, so I joined AA and began to get my life together. Our relationship got pretty serious, so I wasn't totally surprised when he proposed. I selected a beautiful, but not very large, diamond for a ring…

Also, I paid for it.

I couldn't expect too much from a guy who lived with his mom. In fact, Austin and I had moved in with Matthew and his mother. So suddenly we were a very non-traditional family, but it worked. He was sober, I was sober, and life suddenly seemed more manageable.

Plus, I kept getting great occupational opportunities. I got a chance to work on *Renaissance Man* with so many iconic comedians and great actors: director Penny Marshall, Danny DeVito, Gregory Hines, Mark Wahlberg, and Lillo Brancato. In the film, Danny DeVito is a broke Detroit advertising exec who loses his job and ends up as an instructor on a nearby Army base. His task is to increase the basic comprehension skills of eight tough cases. I was one of those hard cases.

Since all of the actors were from New York, we were naturally a little out of our element on set at Jackson Army Base in Columbia, South Carolina. They put us through a "boot camp" as part of a platoon to get us ready for the filming. We were instructed to act as if we were soldiers, but we got in trouble every day: for not wearing our hats, for using profanity, and for generally not following the social protocols of a Southern military base.

We were quite the contrast with the actual soldiers. I loved watching them walk in straight lines, move in unison, and exercise until they were dripping with sweat. (That didn't take long down South.)

It seems that at one point not too long ago, everyone supported the troops. It was natural and right to express appreciation for people who donned the uniform—with flags, yellow ribbons, or a handshake at the airport. Of course, when there's anything that's culturally accepted as "good," the Left has to strike back against it. Now it's fashionable to knock soldiers down a little off their cultural pedestal.

Liberal writers point out isolated abuses at Abu Ghraib and feel they no longer have the moral responsibility to support all soldiers. Professors say we shouldn't go around thanking soldiers just for wearing the camouflage or for fighting in military actions that they don't support.

But there's enough lunacy to go around when it comes to the military. With Obama in the White House, some Republicans say that Christian conservatives shouldn't join the military until we get a better commander in chief. They argue that since religious liberty is under attack in the military—because chaplains are facing discipline for their religious points of view—Americans ought to just stop enlisting.

Give me a break. The military should be a politics-free zone, and all Americans should support them. When I was on that base, I was honored to be able to see what many Americans don't get a chance to witness—men and women who voluntarily make a decision to be willing to lay down their lives for this nation.

Presidents, as unique and frustrating as they may be in their own ways, thankfully don't govern forever. But the courage and self-lessness of our citizens has to be a constant quality of American life. We just can't make it as a nation if there aren't a certain number of people willing to raise their hands and take an oath to protect this country from its enemies. Christians don't get a free pass just because they don't like the guy in charge. It's spine-less and isn't good for our national character. Freedom has been bought at a price—blood—and every American community should take seriously our duty to protect it.

Similarly, military service is an honorable choice that deserves respect no matter how you feel about specific military actions. When you shake a soldier's hand or give up your better seat for him on an airplane, you are honoring something far more transcendent: selflessness and courage that is a necessary ingredient for America's survival.

I don't see a lot of that in Hollywood. So I was glad, in those few months of shooting, to have a front row seat on the best elements of American life.

——

"Are you sitting down?" my agent asked me.

"No, I'm walking to the ocean," I said.

"Where are you?"

"Venice Beach," I said, clutching the gigantic bag that held my sunscreen, my bottles of water, my towel. Matthew was walking a bit in front of me, carrying his surfboard. Strong offshore winds were blowing across the land toward the water, which caused my sundress to whip up around me. The winds were perfect for surfing, according to Matthew, because they caused the waves to break more cleanly and slowly. The waves that day were apparently perfect, which is why we had packed up and headed to the water.

Not that Matthew had much else to do. We'd been dating for two years, and I began to notice that his life basically revolved around surfing and trying to get a gig acting. That was pretty much it. I didn't care much about surfing, so I'd planned on going to the beach and laying out while occasionally pretending to look up and watch him on the waves. Something about my agent's tone of voice told me that my plans for the day were about to change. Maybe even for my whole life. "Why? What's going on?"

"You got it," he said.

It had been just a couple of weeks since he sent me the script with the word "Clueless" on the front. I remember scanning the document, looking specifically for the part for which I was reading. Dionne Davenport. I didn't realize it at the time, but the script was based on Jane Austen's classic 1815 novel *Emma*. Okay, so it was a loose interpretation, but the basic plotlines and characters were there.

The film's main character Cher Horowitz parallels Austen's Emma. But instead of taking place in the early nineteenth-century countryside like the novel, the film is set in a Beverly Hills high school. Like her literary counterpart, Cher is attractive, wealthy, and spoiled. The only trouble in her charmed life happened at a very young age when her mother passed away from liposuction-gone-bad. I don't think that's how it went down in *Emma*.

The character for whom I had auditioned, Dionne, was Cher's well-dressed best friend who's a junior in high school. Together they befriend Tai Frasier, an unknown new girl from Brooklyn, who has an accent, a skater-grunge wardrobe, and a drug habit. In both the novel and the movie, the main character befriends the new girl and introduces her to a higher society. That, of course, calls for a makeover!

Okay, that might not sound like Jane Austen, but the spirit of the movie definitely honors the novel. Austen, after all, described her main character this way: "The real evils, indeed, of Emma's situation were the power of having rather too much her own way, and a disposition to think a little too well of herself." Cher, with her daddy's credit card privileges, thought very well of herself. In fact, she didn't even learn how to park. Why? "What's the point? Everywhere you go has valet," the script read.

I turned the page, and then turned another. Before I even realized it, I was all the way through the script.

I wanted this.

A few days later, I walked into the reading room. I was in front of a table that included Amy Heckerling and Twink Caplan, who are still my friends, and casting directors. I knew Amy already had two great films under her belt: *Fast Times at Ridgemont High* and *Johnny Dangerously*—one of my favorite movies.

She wasn't what I expected. She was from the Bronx and funny as hell. She was ageless, wore black eyeliner, and had great unkempt hair. She wore tights and a black skirt. I could tell immediately that she's a very real and up-front person. Authentic.

I had prepared some lines that reflected the tone of the movie.

They nodded for me to go ahead.

I got this.

This is mine.

I had my sides—the parts of the script that I had prepared to use for the audition—down cold, but I held the papers in my hand anyway. I liked the feel of having them there, and I could refer to them if I needed to.

I did more than read the lines. I inhabited them. And I knew they loved it and loved me.

A few days later, I got a call back. When I went back into the room again, Amy and the producer Scott Rudin wanted me to read lines with other actors who were auditioning for the character of Murray—Dionne's boyfriend.

The first actor was Terrence Howard, who has since been in several movies and even nominated for an Oscar. The second was Donald Faison, an actor from Harlem who had a quick smile and a great spirit (and later became most famous for his role on *Scrubs*). When I read with him, our chemistry was apparent to everyone. Then, on another day, I was called back in to read with Alicia Silverstone, most famous at the time for starring in Aerosmith's "Cryin'" video. Again, we had great chemistry. There were many other people who auditioned for various parts, including Reese Witherspoon (Cher), Jeremy Renner (Christian and Josh), Owen Wilson (Travis), Zooey Deschanel (Amber and Cher), Leah Remini (Tai), Seth Green (Travis), and Lauryn Hill (Dionne). After about four auditions, Amy—who later revealed she was looking for somebody who seemed like royalty for the Dionne character—made her decision.

That's why my agent was calling on that sunny day.

"I got what exactly?"

"The role in *Clueless*. You're going to be Dionne!" he said. "We're going into the negotiations on salary, but I thought you'd like to know."

I turned off my phone and almost fell out in the middle of the street.

"What?" Matthew asked. The driver of a red Mercedes, which had stopped at the crosswalk for us, leaned out of his window to express his impatience.

"Are you going to just live in the crosswalk?" he yelled, "Or can I go to work today?"

I ignored the guy and started jumping up and down.

"Are you okay?" Matthew asked.

"I got the part!" I said, tears rolling down my face. The Mercedes rolled around us, the driver shaking his head. "I got it!"

━━━

I got out of the shower, toweled off, and looked in my closet for some comfortable clothes. It was the first day of shooting, so I didn't have to look good when I arrived. Once I got to the set, they'd send me to hair and makeup first thing. No reason to waste time doing it twice. *These should work*, I thought, slipping on my Ugg shoes, jeans, and a tee shirt, and headed to the studio.

When I arrived, I was led to a "double banger" trailer, which is just a trailer that's been divided into two.

"Nice," I said, as I looked around the lot. In Hollywood, you can tell the importance of the actor by checking out the size of their trailer—a place where they get ready, rest, and have alone time while on set. I looked around—there was a living room, a dining area, a closet, a bathroom with a shower. Other stars were stuck into "triple bangers," which are trailers divided into three parts with three doors. But even they were better than "honey wagons"—trailers divided into four tiny spaces. "This is great," I said after checking out my trailer.

"Would you like breakfast?" the production assistant asked. After taking my request, she ushered me to hair and makeup for about two hours before I was to arrive for my set call. Everyone's call time was the same, so some of the cast would be in hair while the others were in makeup.

When I first got to see the cast that Amy Heckerling had assembled, I realized—Amy's a casting genius! Alicia Silverstone was cast as Cher; Elisa Donovan played Amber Mariens, Cher's nemesis, with a perfectly spiteful air. (She based her character off girls from her high school!) Donald got the part of Murray, and I loved having another actor from New York there. In fact, all of the roles were perfectly cast: Paul Rudd was Josh Lucas, the college freshman son of Cher's father's favorite ex-wife; Breckin Meyer was Travis Birkenstock, a stoner who eventually gives his bongs to charity and goes to rehab; Dan Hedaya was

Cher's lawyer dad, Mel Horowitz; Jeremy Sisto was Elton Tiscia, the object of a matchmaking scheme gone wrong; Wallace Shawn was amazing as Mr. Wendell Hall. This movie taught me that casting is everything. Chemistry is everything. You could hire Brad Pitt and Tom Cruise, but if they don't have chemistry it's not going to work.

Over the course of the three-month shooting, this group of strangers got to know each other so well on the fun and relaxed set that we seemed like family. Amy had such a clear vision, and she was able to translate it to us perfectly. Plus, she knew if an actor required great coaching or needed space. She knew not only how many words to say, but which words to say. She created an atmosphere on the set that I've never seen replicated in all of my years in Hollywood. What moviegoers saw on screen was exactly what happened every day.

When I first arrived on set, the crew set up the shots, and I was given a call sheet. That told me the order of the scenes, which scenes were planned, and what lines we were going to run for that day. The first scene we shot—though it was not the first scene in the movie—was the infamous driving scene. We were driving through Beverly Hills and I had on the *Cat in the Hat* hat.

"Hello, that was a stop sign," I said.

"I totally paused," Alicia—as Cher—said.

It was hilarious.

There was another scene that was incredibly fun to shoot, though—honestly—all of them were fun. In that scene, Dionne was behind the wheel driving Cher and Murray (in his BMW) on the freeway. Amy first thought of doing this scene because she's horrified of driving on the freeway—which is really tough to avoid in Los Angeles. When Amy first got her driver's license, a drunk driver coming off of a freeway hit her and injured her pretty badly. She created that scene to show how scary the freeway is. I think we did a good job conveying that fear!

The car that I was "driving" was attached to a camera truck with a rig on it. The producers put a camera in the car for some shots and one outside of the car for others. During that scene—which took us all day to shoot—we were actually on the freeway. Trucks were going by, we were screaming, and it was fantastic. We had so much fun filming that, because we were so over the top.

And another scene that was pretty memorable was the party scene in which Cher and Dionne take Tai to a party where Cher unsuccessfully tries to play matchmaker for Tai and Elton.

I wasn't in that scene, and I'm glad because it took forever to shoot and it was sort of gross! It was famous for its infamous "Suck and Blow" game. The way the game worked was simple: the first person takes a credit card and inhales to create suction so that the card will stick to their lips. Then they exhale slightly so the card detaches from their mouth and onto the mouth of the next person in line. On film, it looked like a sexy game. If the card slipped, you'd be kissing the next player! But it looked absolutely disgusting to shoot. None of the actors was able to maintain the constant sucking or blowing required to make it work. Props drilled holes in the credit card, but it didn't help.

Finally they created a fake credit card made of a lighter-weight cardboard. After that didn't work, they applied loads of *Chap-Stick*® to the actors' lips to make it stick. Yuck.

Also, they were pumping smoke in from a machine to make everything look more festive. And many of the extras were smoking fake cigarettes, which have a terrible smell and gave everyone headaches.

Another memorable scene was when Donald's character Murray got his head shaved. The producers didn't want him to actually shave all of his hair because they wanted him to be able to shoot other scenes set chronologically before the party—scenes are always shot out of sequence. So at the party they shaved only the top of his head, leaving hair on the sides so he could wear baseball caps and look like he still had hair. When Donald announced that he looked like George Jefferson, Breckin and Paul absolutely cracked up. From that point on, any time they wanted to humble Donald, they'd just knock off his hat and call him George. I loved shooting this scene, because playing Dionne—Murray's girlfriend—I absolutely threw a fit.

"Why did you do this to your head?" I yelled.

"Because I'm keepin' it real."

That line wasn't in the script, but Donald had heard some kid in his neighborhood say it, so he thought he'd try it out. I thought it worked, so we kept going. Amy loved it and kept it in the script. An unplanned aspect of another scene happened by chance, when Amy and I were talking on set and I happened to sneeze.

"That's not for real," she said. "That is the most delicate yet squeaky sneeze I've ever heard."

"Yeah," I said. "It is."

"Okay, we're putting that in," she laughed.

In the movie, I sneezed and Alicia said, "Dee, when your allergies act up, take out your nose ring."

As the director, Heckerling was there every step of the way, watching every move we made and everything we did. "This is what I want," she'd say. Or, "That was good but this wasn't good." Or, "We have to do that!"

The camaraderie was helped by the fact that everyone was really young and excited to be on set. Alicia and Brittany were only eighteen years old at the time, while Donald was twenty-one—they were at least close to the ages of their roles. I, on the other hand, was twenty-seven!

Alicia brought her dog to set and fussed with it all the time.

People would ask, "Hey Stacey, do you have a dog?"

"No," I said. "I have a kid."

"What? You have a child?"

"Yes, I do," I said. "I have a child, not a dog." I guess they were surprised because I was playing a high school student. But by that time Austin was five years old. Even though I didn't look it, I was in a much different stage of life from most of the actors and actresses. I didn't really hang out with the cast except Amy and Twink, who played Miss Geist. That's why it was nice to have my own trailer, where I could focus for the time I was on set. Then I had to go home and be a mommy. My mind was always on different things—babysitting, playdates, ABCs, making ends meet for my son.

Pretty soon, my life settled into a new routine. I'd have to be at the set by 6:00 or 6:30, so I'd get up at 5:00. I'd leave Austin with Matthew and his mother, who would take care of him while I worked. Every day was full of scenes, but the Screen Actors Guild rules say that they have to give you twelve hours off work before they put your next call in. In other words, whenever they wrap, they can call you twelve hours later. If they don't give you enough time—which is called "forcing your call"—they have to ask you if you're willing to come in. The plus side is that they have to pay you more.

Though the schedule was pretty full, it was never monotonous or boring because we had different scenes every day. Plus, each scene required a wardrobe change. In *Clueless* we had so many wardrobe changes that getting all of the clothes tailored to us took almost a week. Every time we put on a new outfit, a wardrobe assistant snapped a Polaroid of us to show to Amy. She ultimately had to approve every outfit, which had to coordinate with what everyone else was wearing.

Costume designer Mona May—a brilliant fashion artist—had her work cut out for her on this film. She said I already knew what kinds of clothes looked good on me and had a developed sense of style, probably because I was older than everyone else. She created wardrobes from scratch for the others and then taught them how to wear these amazing clothes none of us could have afforded. In fact, Mona's fashions defined the movie even though style in the 1990s was a little suspect. Back then, kids wore flannel shirts, drab jackets, ratty jeans with holes so they could let their long johns show. They tried to replicate the industrial look of Kurt

Cobain and Courtney Love by digging through the offerings at their local thrift stores. This could've been a reaction to the 1980s, when hair was almost an architectural feat—defying gravity with its high poofs and "wings" on the sides. In the 1990s, no one seemed to own a brush or care about high fashion.

But Mona turned that grunginess on its head. Inspired by her European roots, she took the high fashion world and adapted it to fit normal teenage bodies in a beautiful, feminine way. Her pieces included knee-high and thigh-high stockings, berets, and Mary Janes. In fact, I still love wearing thigh-high stockings, and put them on every chance I get!

In the 1980s, I was a punk rocker, so all that plaid was especially great. I loved the thigh-highs and the shoes, but the hats were just stunning. Women just haven't worn hats since the 60s so those hats became characters unto themselves. Though some say mine may have looked like they were inspired by Dr. Seuss, they worked. Plus, they made me feel glamorous.

In this film, Alicia had sixty outfit changes, and I had fifty.

"Why do we need this many clothes?" Alicia complained during about the thirty-seventh fitting, but I always loved it. Ever since I was a teenager—maybe before—I loved fashions and designers. Of course, when Alicia saw the film, she understood the costume requirements. The film inspired the clothing of the last half of the 90s. *Vogue* named our movie the "fashion movie of the year," and the *New York Times* said that it was "best enjoyed as an extended fashion show."

But as visually stunning as the costumes were, the script was just as dazzling.

Whatever was said in this movie just seemed to catch on in pop culture. Some of Cher's lines were so funny and memorable. For example:

"You see how picky I am about my shoes, and they only go on my feet," explaining why she's a virgin.

"Do you prefer 'fashion victim,' or 'ensembly challenged'?"

"Dionne and I were both named after great singers of the past, who now do infomercials."

But my favorite line in the whole movie belonged to me. When Amber was complaining in physical education class, she said, "My plastic surgeon doesn't want me doing any activity where balls fly at my nose."

I immediately replied, "Well, there goes your social life."

To this day, people will come up to me and say that line—I always laugh.

Amy had a great ear for the way teenagers back then were talking, but she earned it. She went to classes, plays, and debates at Beverly Hills High School, to skateboarding contests, and to clothing stores so she could eavesdrop on conversations that kids were having at the time. The resulting script revealed this California Beverly Hills lingo to America. For the first time, people heard the *Clueless* lexicon, which then became a major part of every teenspeak. If you watch the movie now, you can't really appreciate the innovative slang—because much of it has become such an ingrained part of our language. (Sort of like watching the original *Star Wars* isn't as impressive now, since they forged the path in special effects!) But here are several phrases and words that *Clueless* introduced to the culture:

CLUELESS DICTIONARY

Whatever (*exclamation*): a dismissive word used to end an argument or indicate a lack of interest in continuing the conversation

As if (*conjunctional phrase*): a phrase that means "there's no way I'm going to do that"

Baldwin (*noun*, but can also be used as an *adjective*): a guy who raises your social status if you date him

Betty and Barney (*nouns*): a pretty girl and an ugly guy

Postal (*adjective*): crazy, nutty

Hello! (*exclamation*, but not a greeting): did you hear me? Are you listening?

Jeepin' (*gerund*): cheating

Monet (*noun*): someone who looks good from afar, but—like the impressionist paintings—is a big mess up close

Totally (*adverb*): completely

Buggin' (*adjective*): upset or confused

Bonehead (*noun*): an idiot

Keepin' it real (*phrase*): used to say you aren't putting on airs or pretending to be more than you are.

The movie came out a year after we wrapped. Our premiere was in Malibu, just down the Pacific Coast Highway on the beach, and I bought a red Chinese dress cut off really short into a mini dress. When I arrived—with Matthew—the energy was electric. Members of the press were everywhere, so reporters would call out my name as I walked by to ask me questions about filming the movie. MTV set up on location, with Daisy

Fuentes and Jenny McCarthy doing on-the-sand interviews with the celebrities. Luscious Jackson, a popular band in the 90s, performed on the beach while people served food and drink to partygoers from colorful striped cabanas.

But the real magic happened when they began showing the film. It was exhilarating to hear everyone laughing so hard. I could tell this film was going to be a huge hit.

It was.

The movie took the box office by storm and became a cultural milestone.

With the success of the movie, I was made into a Barbie. Yes, you read that correctly: I am a Barbie doll. At the time, I didn't buy one, an oversight I regretted twelve years later, when I had my daughter Lola. Thank God for eBay!

I loved it because Dionne, Cher, and Tai were not brats, we just had very strong opinions. We weren't "mean girls" (like the protagonists in the later Lindsay Lohan movie), we just knew what we wanted and knew how things should be. We had confidence in our taste and values: we didn't smoke pot, didn't hang out with the druggies (even though we were friendly toward them), and we didn't have sex. Now, when I see my daughter Lola taking a *Clueless* nightgown to every sleepover, I smile.

This movie changed my life and gave me many opportunities. I have to thank Amy Heckerling once again. No movie got it so right before *Clueless*, and no movie has gotten it quite as right since.

ELEVEN

GOD'S WAY

Let me not to the marriage of true minds
Admit impediments, love is not love
Which alters when it alteration finds,
Or bends with the remover to remove.
O no, it is an ever-fixed mark
That looks on tempests and is never shaken;
It is the star to every wand'ring bark,
Whose worth's unknown, although his height be taken.
Love's not Time's fool, though rosy lips and cheeks
Within his bending sickle's compass come,
Love alters not with his brief hours and weeks,
But bears it out even to the edge of doom:
If this be error and upon me proved,
I never writ, nor no man ever loved.

—William Shakespeare

With the success of *Clueless*, we had the opportunity to film a television series spin off. (The only two cast members from the movie who didn't sign up with the show were Alicia and Brittany. Alicia went to the Amazon River with Woody Harrelson to help save the rain forest. Brittany pursued other movie roles.) I looked forward to reuniting with this fun group of actors. Plus, the regular paycheck wouldn't be bad, either. I was still living with Matthew and his mom. Matthew was still surfing, and he had yet to drop the "aspiring" from his description of "aspiring actor." In fact, he never worked, so I had to bring in all the income.

On the first day of the series, we were on the Paramount lot shooting an outdoor scene when I noticed a guy who looked a lot like Matt Damon. He was the "Best Boy," which is someone who sets up the shots and makes sure everything is lit appropriately.

"I want a light here on this," he said, asking someone to rig a light.

Our eyes met and he just kept staring at me and watching every move I made. Finally Kevin got up his nerve to say something to me. He popped his head into my trailer and said, "Do you want to go see a movie or something?" That's how the flirting commenced.

One day, Matthew brought Austin by to see the set. When Kevin saw that Austin was there, he came to my trailer. "I want to meet your son," he said, without regard to the fact that Matthew—who was still my fiancé—was there. Kevin and Austin really hit it off. A few days later, we actually went to a movie. I remember *Tin Cup* was playing, but we barely made it through the opening credits. We ended up going to a Holiday Inn, and that was it.

"Will you and Austin move in with me?" he asked, as we lay there in the hotel room.

The next day at work, we were openly flirting with each other. Everybody knew my situation—that I was the one making the money while engaged to a surfer who lived with his mother. It was no surprise when Kevin and I started dating. Well…no one was surprised except Matt. He was devastated. I gave him back his ring, got Austin, and moved into Kevin's two-bedroom apartment. He bought Austin a bunk bed and made a little boy's room for him.

Kevin loved my son so much and was ready for the role of Dad. He proposed right away. Eventually he and I had a big Catholic wedding and bought a house out in Thousand Oaks so we could be near his mom. I loved his family, and his family loved me. I made a lot of money for three years. The show took twelve- to fifteen-hour days, five days a week to shoot. His mom kept Austin while Kevin and I worked. We got to see each other all day every day. It was awesome! But I was driving from Thousand Oaks to Paramount Studios, which is like an hour and a half drive every day back and forth. I'd have to be at work by 6:00 in the morning, I wouldn't get off until 7:00 or 8:00, and I wouldn't get home until 10:00 at night. So I barely got to see Austin. I think that put a lot of stress on our marriage.

Then when *Clueless* the series stopped, so did our income. Kevin wasn't working, and we were suddenly in over our heads. And we were living in the middle of nowhere. Though our home was in a lovely neighborhood, it was about thirty-five miles from downtown Los Angeles. I'm a city girl, so I was bored to tears. I just couldn't do it anymore.

"Maybe that's the problem," he offered. "Let's move to the Hollywood Hills and be right in the middle of everything!" And so we sold our house and rented a nice home in the hills. We tried to make it work, but a change of location wasn't enough to save us.

When I began packing Austin's clothes, Kevin simply wouldn't accept what I was saying. We had been together five years, though the marriage had lasted just a year. In spite of his protests, we remained friends, but the divorce was pretty devastating to both of us. Of all my broken relationships, this is the one that still burns. He was a great guy and a great husband. He loved Austin. In fact, Austin still considers Kevin his father. I still call him if anything happens, and he's immediately there for me.

My main problem with Kevin wasn't a problem with Kevin after all. It was a problem with me. I had never seen what "domesticity" looked like. When you grow up in front of a television in the South Bronx, raised by drugs addicts, it's honestly hard to know how to be a good wife. When I'm out in public and see families hanging out with each other, I always marvel at their casual affection and interactions. I just don't know what it's like. The closest thing to a functioning family I had was my grandparents' life-long marriage…which itself was rife with affairs. Infidelity and broken families perpetuate themselves. That's the thing.

I really wish that marriage could've worked. At the time, I didn't understand what love was. I still don't understand.

Austin and I moved to Sunset Plaza. I used the money I'd made on the show and lived a little bit of a freewheeling "single life." Well, as freewheeling as you can be with a child. I met a woman named Linda who introduced me to her set of British pals, and suddenly I had a group of friends with incredibly cool accents. One night we were at a restaurant called Tangier when a man I had never seen walked in.

"This is George, everyone," said our friend Dorian. "He's staying with me on his way to Hong Kong."

"I'm on a layover," he said to me, seeming to think that he needed to explain his presence in our otherwise tight group. George carried himself like an upper class Englishman. Over the course of dinner, I discovered that he had gone to Eton College, Britain's most famous boarding school, in the shadow of Windsor Castle. There young men network with the sons of their fathers' friends, learn to use the proper grammar, charm the right ladies, and prepare themselves for a possible life on Downing Street. The school has educated nineteen prime ministers—including David Cameron—and George confided that he was a third-generation Etonian.

"So why aren't you prime minister yet?" I asked.

"Someone has to do sports marketing," he laughed. That's exactly what he did, for big world events like the World Cup, cricket, rugby, and soccer. He was traveling to Hong Kong for an event the very next day.

We stayed together all night and bonded immediately. After our night together, we dreamed about one day having a baby. I have no idea why we started down that line of thought, other than just the headiness and novelty of a new relationship.

"If we had a little girl," I said aloud, "what would we name her?"

"Lola."

That's how I met my second husband, and that's how we chose the name of our—eventual—daughter.

A lot can happen in a layover.

He left on Sunday to go to Hong Kong, and three days later my phone rang. "Will you come meet me?"

"Where are you?"

"I can't stop thinking of you."

So I went to Hong Kong for a memorable few days.

"That's it," he said. "It's you and me. You're my girlfriend."

One night, about three months later, we were making love. Just at the climax, he put a ring on my finger.

And it was a big one.

The ring, that is.

I looked at the four carats on my hand and smiled. "I do."

Three months later, I drove him to the airport to take him to a business trip. We couldn't keep our hands off of each other. Finally, I pulled over at the Airport Hilton near LAX and we got a room, which we used for about an hour. Soon, I found out I was pregnant...a sort of self-fulfilling prophecy.

"We have to delay the wedding," I said. "I'm not walking down the aisle pregnant."

George belonged to the Church of England, and he had told me of a special place in Britain where he wanted to get married. "We can just delay it," I said.

Over the next nine months, we had a lot of work to do. We decided to set up house in Los Angeles. We bought all our furniture in South Africa and had it shipped home. When it arrived, I had a month to go before my due date.

We were unloading the beautiful furniture, putting it in the house, and dreaming of what our new home would look like.

"Uh-oh," I said, looking down at my leg.

"Did your water just break?"

"No, I'm just leaking fluid," I said. I dismissed it, because it was little bits of fluid that came throughout the day. It was easy to ignore with all of the unpacking and decorating.

About 9:30 at night, I finally called my doctor. "I've been leaking fluid all day."

"What do you mean, 'all day'?" he said, the sound of sleep thick in his voice. "Why didn't you call me earlier? Get to the hospital right now."

"You can't hold onto this baby," my doctor said after checking me. "If we don't induce you, you'll have to be on bed rest."

He gave me medicine to sleep, and we selected a time for her birth: 5:25 p.m., June 21—the same birthday as Prince William. George, my mother, my best friend Cynthia, and Austin were there in the room when little Lola made her debut. George and Austin cut her umbilical cord together. I could barely contain myself. I finally felt that my family was complete.

We were so happy...for about two years. Then we began fighting more and more. Regardless, we thought we could make our family work, so we decided to go ahead and marry. The idea held less magic than it once had for me. Our relationship seemed to have already run its course. Though I loved George—and still do—it simply didn't seem to be working between us. But family was so important, we wanted to make it work. For our daughter's sake.

"What should we do to get married?" he asked as we sat around the house one night. Lola was already asleep in her crib, and we realized that we'd neglected to deal with this detail of life. The church wedding didn't seem like a good idea.

"Let's go to Vegas," he said, which sounded fun at the time. How many people have gotten hitched there, taken by a bit of spontaneity and romance? Turns out, it wasn't as ideal as I'd hoped. We went to one of those ugly little chapels, he walked ten feet in front of me the whole time, and we got back on the plane as man and wife. It was a way to tie the knot without very much fuss, without very much fanfare.

If you're trying to have a wedding with as little effort as possible, that's probably a sign that it shouldn't happen. When Lola was barely able to communicate ideas, she stood between us during one particularly cruel fight. "Don't talk to my mommy that way," she said to her father. We were divorced three years later.

After the divorce, I moved with Austin and Lola into a teeny eight-hundred-square-feet apartment. I shared a bedroom with Lola, who still slept in a crib even though she was three. Austin's room was right next door. By this time, he was a teenager! Though cramped, it worked for us. I needed to get away. From men. From expectations. From everything.

I guess I should go ahead and tell you that precisely zero of my marriages worked out. And I wasn't done yet.

After my divorce from George, I made a proclamation. "I don't want a man, I'm never gonna see a man, I don't want to think about a man," I told my manager over the phone. "I'm focusing on my career."

Within eight months, I was engaged to an Italian actor named Francesco, who'd had roles in some major films. I found him irresistible and charming—until he wasn't. After two years of his unemployment, the bloom came off this rose as well.

"Okay, this is not working for me," I said. "I can't do this. You have to get a real job, the kind that pays money." Instead of pursuing acting, he got a real estate license and began establishing a business there in Los Angeles. He tried, but we'd gotten down to our last dime.

"I need $3,000," I said into the phone to my business manager. I was at Saks and had found a perfect dress.

"Um, Stacey, I'm not sure how to tell you this, but…" My business manager sighed. I could tell this was hard on him, but I was about to have a hard time if I didn't get to buy this dress. "You just don't have it."

"I have it, Don," I insisted. "I've worked my ass off, I know I've got the money." It felt like every time I called my business manager I was met with hesitation and mumbled apologies. But that day it was different.

"Stacey, this is Gina," said an unfamiliar voice on the line. She spoke with confidence and authority, as if she had earned the money and had full rights over the way it was divvied up. "I can't give you $3,000, but I can give you $1,500."

I paused for a moment. "Who the hell are you?"

It was an interesting question. Gina, in her career, had toured with NSYNC, Toni Braxton, Reba McEntire, Britney Spears, and Janet Jackson and had assisted Shanice Wilson, the first African American to play Eponine in *Les Misérables* on Broadway. She had handled finances for Pat Boone, Matthew Hines, Cuba Gooding Jr., Jennifer Aniston, Elise Neal, Juliette Lewis, and more. I met her right after she'd decided to quit the business, except for a short stint to help out with the estate of Michael Jackson after his death. For a few days, she was neck deep in organizing his materials for the court hearing. Every single time I called, she noticed how my handlers panicked. They didn't know how to say no to me.

She had seen my movies, so she was familiar with the roles I'd played...but she didn't connect my name to the person on the phone. Gina wasn't bothered at all to tell me that I wasn't going to get money. "You don't have it, so I can't give it," she'd say, matter-of-factly. I respected the woman. Later that day, I called my manager and he simply passed the phone to Gina.

"Do you realize your tags on the BMW are expired and your driver's license is too?" she asked.

"No they're not," I said, before realizing she was exactly right.

"Just meet me at the DMV," she said with the same confidence as when she was telling me I couldn't have my money. She had a certain manner that made me want to do what she said. And I rarely have that feeling with anyone. When I got to the DMV, I came face to face with Gina. She was a little Mexican woman with green eyes who seemed to know everything about my bills and personal files. True to her word, she took care of my license and vehicle. On our way out, I mentioned that my phone was acting up.

"Let's go to the phone store and check on your plan."

That was how I met the woman who would take care of me...possibly the only woman to ever consistently take care of me in my life. She began helping my business manager part time and then would stop by my house and work until 5:00 in the afternoon or so. There, she'd take care of everything. If she noticed dimmed light bulbs, the next thing I knew she'd be teetering on a ladder replacing them. She made sure that all of the little household annoyances were taken care of before I even noticed that they needed attention. She tried to make sure she was gone before Francesco came home, because he found her suspicious.

"Why is she working for free?" he asked me one night as we got into the bed. I didn't know. I just knew that I valued her so much that I hoped she'd stick around. "It just feels like she's after something."

One day, Francesco came home and saw Gina on her way out of the house carrying clothes to take to the cleaners.

"The next thing I know I'll come home and you'll be in bed with my wife," he said.

"No thank you, but if you don't take her car to get the oil changed soon, I will," she said as she walked out the door.

Turns out, Gina did have an ulterior motive. Things started getting really shady with Francesco, and I began to fear that he just wasn't right. Eventually, he got abusive too. But I was done letting guys use me as their punching bag. I went to the police, filed a report, and got a restraining order. I had no job—and even less money than I thought. Turns out, Francesco hadn't paid the rent on our house for three months.

The day the restraining order was granted—requiring he stay one hundred yards away from the kids, our home, and me—I filed for divorce. I had hit rock bottom, with no real options for getting back up.

Turns out, Gina knew all along. When she had started to look into my finances, she realized that Francesco was bad news. She knew he was in over his head, that he had been "robbing Peter to pay Paul," and that I was headed for financial ruin. I guess she didn't want me to go through it alone. And so she worked quietly, waiting for the moment when the truth would come out. It always does, eventually.

Gina, God love her, still stuck around even though I had less than no money to pay her. By the time Francesco left, we'd gotten to be friends—almost like family. I was determined to make enough money to start paying her. But how?

"Why don't you do a reality show about your life?" my brother suggested. It sounded like a reasonable idea. Honestly,

I had never met anyone with a life quite as dramatic as mine. We put together a sizzle reel—a video presentation of what my show would look like—and VH1 loved it. But it would take a while to determine if they actually wanted to buy it.

About a month after Francesco left, Gina walked into the house holding a piece of paper.

"This was on your front door," she said. It was a handwritten "3 Days or Quit" notice. This is what California has decided landlords must do to give notice to occupants who haven't paid their rent in too long. It had the name and address of my landlord and said that I'd have to move out if I didn't pay in three days.

"I bet all my neighbors saw that!" I wailed. "What are we going to do?"

"Well, we've got three days," Gina said. "It's not over yet."

One day after this notice, I got an audition. VH1 was producing their first scripted show, and I auditioned for it at their request.

"Listen, we love you for the lead," the head of VH1 said. "Please reconsider the reality television route. Wouldn't you rather do this scripted show instead of the reality one?" The new show, produced by Queen Latifah, was called *Single Ladies*. I didn't have a great feeling about it, but I needed the money. "Let me put it to you this way. Do you want to be Kim Kardashian or Carrie Bradshaw?" he asked, implying that scripted roles carry more prestige. I looked up at the ceiling as I tried to weigh my options. Turns out, I didn't really have any options. "Plus there's this. If you don't do the scripted show, we're not gonna do your reality show."

In other words, he was holding my reality TV show hostage. Without a real alternative, I agreed to be the lead in *Single Ladies*. After I shot the pilot, I met a guy named Max, a very wealthy man from Texas who lived in Copenhagen. He was in the process of getting a divorce from his wife. They'd been separated for a while, so the legal divorce was just a formality. After we met, he called me and said that he had literally turned his plane around to come back to see me.

"Please come to New York," he asked. "It's a great place to be over the Fourth of July, and I have to be there for business."

After our wonderful weekend in New York, he asked me to meet him in France. Paris is the City of Lights, but it's also a city for lovers. Max and I made love there for the first time. It was so romantic, and I couldn't believe how deeply I felt for him after such a short time. I spent the entire time in Paris at the hotel, waiting for him to show up to see me. In fact, I never left the hotel while he was at his business meetings.

"I want to see Paris!" I said, grabbing his arm after days of room service. I wanted to go shopping for shoes, to experience the most romantic city on earth.

"Listen," Max said. "I have something to tell you. We can't go out." Apparently, he was worried that word would get out that we were lovers.

"Are you ashamed of me?"

"Well, I wouldn't want my wife to find out."

"She has to face facts eventually," I said. "You're separated."

"Well, we're still *technically* together."

"What do you mean *technically*?" I said.

"We're not quite separated," he smiled. "We're nesting."

"You're birds now?"

"I live in the downstairs and she lives upstairs," he explained. "That way, the kids don't have to switch between both of our homes."

"You don't want her to know about me?"

Something wasn't adding up. I left him at the hotel, feeling betrayed. Max had lied to me. I walked down the cobblestoned streets of Paris, looking at the lovers walking hand in hand right next to the River Seine. Bicycles with baskets leaned against lampposts, stylish women carrying large shopping bags stopped at cafes for a snack. The city was alive and vibrant, but I felt dead inside.

This is never going to work, I thought. *I should stop this now. I shouldn't go any further.* But there was one small problem. I had already made love to him—a married man! Suddenly, I was "the other woman" again—something I had never wanted to be again since I cheated with Axel. I felt that I loved him. No, it was more than just a feeling. I did love him.

And because of that feeling, I stayed with Max, and hoped that his divorce would work out soon enough.

Within weeks, I found out the pilot for *Single Ladies* had been successful. The show had been picked up, so Lola and I moved to Atlanta to start shooting. Though I have had trouble keeping my personal life in order, I'm a consummate professional at work. I'm on set, on time. I know my lines. I can give you an eight-hour day or a twelve-hour day with no problem. But many of the other actresses and actors on the set didn't have the same idea about work. The acting was horrible, the plot was raunchy, and the hours were long. No matter how late we stayed up the night before, I was always on time. If we had to be there at 7:30, Gina and I were there at 7:00. Meanwhile, everybody else got there at 8:15 or 8:30 and still needed three hours to do hair. Most of the other girls had black hair, which takes a lot longer to do than Latin hair. I'd end up waiting for hours in my trailer.

I actually had an actress come up to me and say, "You wash your hair every day like a white girl, don't you?"

Holy shit. She actually said this to me.

The topic of hair amongst black women is one of the most hotly contested, debated, divisive topics you can imagine. Black women try to stick everyone into different camps—on one side are the "big hair don't care" ladies who believe in "natural hair." On the other are ladies who use chemical relaxers to straighten their hair and make it easier to deal with. When the topic of hair comes up, you can immediately see black women's eyes light up. The "natural hair" women whip their hair back and forth and explain that they love how God made them. The "relaxed hair" women say that their lives are easier because God gave them chemicals for a reason. Black women judge each other on their hair more than on any other topic—even the phrase "good hair" is now considered an insult. What *is* good hair, after all? Is there an element of racism in that phrase, because it implies that looser curls are somehow better than kinky hair? The politics of black women's hair cannot be solved by any amount of debate or reason. If you're not a black woman, you have no idea the contention and judgment black women hoist on each other. (Though

Chris Rock did a good job trying to understand it in his movie, *Good Hair*.)

I, however, am on the outside of this debate. I find it boring and small. Because I'm half black and half Mexican, my hair texture is different from everyone else's. Black women will sometimes take one look at my hair and immediately try to classify me as "not black enough."

On the set of *Clueless*, my hair was discussed by the stylists on the very first day.

"You've got great hair," said one after I settled into the chair. She held some of my hair in her hand and examined it. It was still damp from my morning shower. "But it won't do," she said as she twirled a lock of it between her fingers.

"I thought you just said it was great."

"It *is* great," she replied, "but it's not black enough."

"Not black enough?" I knew instantly what she meant. "What about braids?" I suggested.

We agreed that braids would do the trick, so I went to a hairstylist who was a friend of mine. She used real hair for the braids, which took six or seven hours to put in, and I had to repeat that every month. Because I washed my hair every day, they didn't last as long as they could've.

As I walked out of hair and makeup, I felt the weight of my new hair on my head. I had to admit I loved the way I looked.

I wasn't offended when she said that my hair "wasn't black enough." Of course, filmmakers have ideas in their heads about "what black people do" and "what black people look like," and it's not bad for actors to change to meet the requirements of a role. However, it does get old when it seeps into real life. My entire life I've been told, I had to behave a certain way, look a certain way, and think a certain way. I was always told I acted like a white girl because of the way I spoke, looked, or washed my hair.

What does that mean, "like a white girl"? I thought when that actress on *Single Ladies* made the snide remark about washing my hair every day. *Do white people have a monopoly on washing their hair? Is that what you're saying?*

But I didn't respond. I could tell the actress was trying to goad me, so I simply put my earbuds in and ignored her.

Gina, who always was standing nearby to monitor things, said, "Oh, well, she's Mexican."

Thankfully, Max was a fun distraction. I saw him about every five days. Wherever he traveled, he wanted me by his side. We went to Copenhagen, New York, Chicago, everywhere. Though I didn't love him for his money, there were benefits. He bought me a six-bedroom house *and* gave me money to decorate it. We spent hours talking about love and life. Frequently, our conversation turned to politics.

Once we were having a conversation about how liberals believe that justice demands that you take money from one group of people and give it to another.

"That's socialism!" I protested.

"Of course," he laughed. "What do you think it is?"

"Oh my God. No, no," I said. "That can't happen. We can't have a socialist nation."

He touched my nose and smiled. "My dear, I believe you are a Republican capitalist."

The more time I spent with Max, the more I learned about politics and the more conservative I realized I am. And I started talking to my friends about such matters...for better or worse. Once I was hanging out with my British friends when I started talking about the opportunities available in America. "I just think it's great that the American dream is available to everyone."

"You can't just keep on saying things like that, you know," my friend Roman said, before taking a long sip of his pinot noir and smiling in my direction.

"Now I'm getting lectured by a Brit about my own damn country?" Everyone laughed.

"The American dream isn't available for *everyone*," he said. "There isn't enough to go around."

"That's an absurd thought. You're putting a limit on the universe? You're putting a limit on God? Anything is possible if you want it."

"Wow, you sound like every Disney movie ever made," he quipped.

For some reason, his line of reasoning angered me.

"You can't tell the difference between Mickey Mouse and Margaret Thatcher. You think you can only get to a certain level of wealth and that's it?" I asked. Wealth isn't like a jar of jelly beans: once you give them away, they're gone. It's more like literacy or life expectancy. It can increase in one area without necessarily decreasing somewhere else. When someone hits it big somewhere in America, he's not taking money out of my pocket. He's generating income, creating it from scratch. That's quite a feat, and I hate how people stoke the bitterness and jealousy of one segment of the population toward the segment that is actually out there making jobs.

People aren't poor because other people are rich. I saw the effects of that line of thinking in the South Bronx. People who get on the dole never get off, they aren't respected, and they end up being someone's bitch. It's obvious welfare has encouraged inefficiency, waste, and laziness. I honestly believe if I could take my friends from the Los Angeles gangs and show them this principle, they'd stop being so resentful of "the Man" keeping them down. Also, if Americans had a better understanding of this notion, they would have respected Mitt Romney for being able to create wealth instead of looking down on him. "Of course you believe this way. You live in Laurel Canyon and don't work," I said. "You borrow money from everybody, so you're used to getting something for nothing. How can I expect you to know about actually creating something instead of just tearing it down? Who the fuck do you think you are?"

The host of the event put her hand up, like a cop directing traffic. "Okay, that's enough," she said. "We're just trying to have a nice dinner. Why don't I go check on the cake in the kitchen?"

"I hope you don't teach this to your children," I said, ignoring the hostess. "Because God forbid they dream."

"Leave my kids out of this," he said.

"This is *about* our kids. We're talking about America's future, but you're buying into the very lie that Democrats tell you to believe. They want you to believe that there's only so much money and those greedy capitalists are stealing it from the average guy on the street. As long as they give you money and you take it, they control you because they control the resources. It's a plantation mentality, and it's not right. I like to call it the 'White House Plantation Mentality.'"

I got up from the table and just walked away, leaving my confused friends sitting there with their mouths slightly open.

If blacks get more wealth, it's because whites must give it up to them. That's what I've heard my whole life. It's a false choice and—frankly—it's degrading. I took my conversation with Roman personally, because his way of thinking undermines black people's achievements and animates much of the racial tension that exists today.

We don't have to choose between blacks and whites, between the *haves* and the *have nots*. We can all choose to act in ways that benefit everyone. That, of course, is capitalism. Everyone knows money doesn't grow on trees. But what Democratic black voters don't get is that money doesn't just fall out of Uncle Sam's pocket. It has to be created. What makes it? People. If people are the ones who generate money by using their minds and their creativity, that means that there's a tremendous amount of hope and possibility right there in the inner city.

In America, our greatest natural resource is the talent of our people. But Democrats hand out dimes and nickels, pat us on the head, and then pack us up in buses to tell us how to vote. It's a shame, and there's nothing that angers me more than a wealthy white liberal spreading the same lies as Al fucking Sharpton.

My friends and I began having very heated political conversations, as something inside of me had awakened. I was a black conservative. No, I was an American. I happened to be black and I happened to be a conservative. But as an American I felt I had the responsibility to talk about these political issues that affect us every day.

The stress of shooting *Single Ladies* was getting to me. I was disappointed in the script, and I didn't enjoy my castmates as much as I had on other shows. Though I loved seeing Max every five days, the international travel was physically taxing.

On Valentine's Day, he asked me to meet him in San Francisco. When I saw him, I could tell there was something odd, something different about him. I'm not sure if he looked different or just was acting different, but certainly something had shifted.

"Do you have something to tell me?" I asked.

"Like what?"

"Like that you've been with someone."

He took my hand and smiled. "You're a paranoid one, aren't you?"

We spent the next five days together, and I couldn't shake the feeling.

"Just tell me," I said. "I need to know."

He assured me, once again, that he hadn't been with anyone else. And so I tried to shake the feeling off, but it lingered like a fly buzzing around my head. I couldn't concentrate without dealing with that annoyance.

"If you ask me about being unfaithful again, I'm gonna leave," he said, after I brought it up once again.

He was so confident and so persuasive. Was he telling the truth? But on the flight home I started feeling weird. I readjusted in my seat, but I felt itchy and uncomfortable. Something wasn't right.

"Gina," I said into the phone. "Make an appointment with Dr. Owens as soon as I land."

I went from LAX to the doctor's office, scared about how I was feeling. After a physical exam and some tests, he came into the room and tossed some antibiotics on the table.

"It looks like you have an STD," he said. "Trichomoniasis."

"What?" I instantly began crying. "How?"

The doctor explained that my sexual partner must have recently contracted an STD, but that it rarely shows symptoms in men. When Max passed it to me, it was a sign that he'd been cheating on me. Just as I'd figured. I wept and wept. My doctor put a hand on my shoulder, awkwardly. As he stood there watching me sob, he finally said, "Stacey, do you think I might need to sedate you?"

He smiled, but I don't think he was joking. In my life, men have come and gone. In every circumstance, I was the one who left them. I'd fall fast for men, but tire of them almost as quickly. But I loved Max and had finally found a long-term partner...or so I thought.

"How could he do this to me?" I said.

"It's a little outside my area of expertise," he said, shrugging. "But I think you need to have a talk with your partner."

The medicine took the pain and itchiness away, but the pain in my heart lingered. Especially when Max admitted the affair. He begged me to give him another chance and made a grand show of his love by taking me to Italy for Easter. There we had a private mass at the Vatican. Then we went to Florence, to the Medici Castle. After our whirlwind European tour, we came back to the United States, to what had become our normal lives. We hosted a party, and while people milled around we walked outside and stood on the edge of a river that ran through the property behind our house. It was so picturesque. We held hands, and I felt like he deserved another chance. After all, we all make mistakes.

While we were standing there, he began talking more philo-sophically. "My life is like the rocky points in the river...." I can't remember the rest of his analogy, mainly because what he said next just simply didn't make sense. He told me that he was the type of man who has affairs. Not that he had an affair, but that he has affairs. Plural.

"Why don't you just look the other way?"

I stood there speechless. I had been with this man for two and a half years, during which time he'd told me repeatedly that he was getting a divorce. Turns out, he wasn't getting a divorce at all, and his wife was not too happy to hear about me. I was standing at the house—our home that I'd set up for the four of us—when he laid this news on me. I was welcome to stay with him, but I'd have to be okay with his constant infidelity. Oh, and his wife.

"Basically you're asking me to be a gold-digging whore?"

"I'm saying things could be easier for you if you just give me some space."

But "some space" meant simply that he'd have sex with as many women as he wanted. All I had to do was pretend it wasn't happening. Then, all of this—the house, the river, the cars, the vacations—could still be mine.

"I don't want to have to use a condom every time we have sex because I'm worried you'll give me an STD!!"

"I'll use a condom with the other women," he had the gall to suggest.

I'm sure my mouth fell open. I'd never been propositioned in this way. And that's what it felt like. A proposition. I wasn't interested in being a prostitute. I wasn't even interested in being "the other woman." I wanted to love Max, and I wanted Max to love me. I wanted someone to help me create a family, a place of security and peace. Instead of explaining to him that I actually loved him—that this had been no act for me—I slapped the shit out of him...so hard he almost fell into his river. His friends, who were standing around sipping on champagne, suddenly got quiet and watched us.

"I don't want your money. Take your fucking house, take your cash, take everything. I don't want it!"

"Have it your way," He said, rubbing his hand over his face. "I'm not going to finance you anymore." At the time, I had some money from work, but definitely not enough to pay the bills for a house with six bedrooms.

"There's no way I can pay for this alone," I said.

"I'll pay one year of rent so that you can get back on your feet and do it on your own. Or, if you're willing to look the other way..." He lightly touched my chin and made me look up at him. "You could keep it."

"Fuck you!" To suddenly find out that he was actually cheating on me, throughout all of my waiting—was overwhelming. But to realize that I'd lose my financial stability if I didn't "look the other way" was downright insulting.

"How will you live?" he asked.

"How could you do this to me?" I screamed. By this time, no one at the party was pretending not to listen. We had a full audience, but I didn't care. "To Lola?"

"I'll pay a year's worth of rent," he offered again. "So you've got a little time to get your life together."

Your life, he'd said. He used to say *our lives*. But I guess he used to be lying. Meanwhile, the atmosphere at *Single Ladies* had grown worse. Conflict on the set, a terrible script, and lots of drama made that scene unbearable. I was on the first full season, but decided not to come back for the second.

I was so devastated by my breakup that I couldn't get out of bed for six months. Gina worried about me, but there was nothing that could be done. My heart had been broken. To make matters worse, I got a notice that I had to get out of my home in five days. Apparently, Max had paid for the year's rent, but that didn't mean I had a year to figure out Plan B. Sooner than I was ready, the year was up, and the landlord wanted another year's contract…in advance. I couldn't pay that. After frantically looking for a place to move, I came up empty. There were not many affordable places to rent for my family of three in Los Angeles, which is where I needed to live to take advantage of job opportunities. And speaking of jobs, I was at a *Clueless* event when someone came up to me and handed me an envelope. "Sign here, please."

In front of the media and fans, I was served a subpoena. I signed my name and laughed, as if this man was just another fan who wanted my autograph. But the truth was far darker. Apparently, Max and his wife finally did get a divorce, and she wanted me in court to help make her case against him. I called Max, afraid of the ramifications of this subpoena, but he assured me I didn't have to go.

With that little piece of advice, Max caused me to be in contempt of court. Not showing up was the most asinine thing I've ever done, since I had nothing to hide. I certainly didn't care to protect him. But suddenly I had to pay a lawyer to help me deal with the legal bills from being in contempt.

"I'm sorry, Stacey," Max said. "I'll reimburse you for the lawyer."

Of course, he never paid one dime. And I sank further into debt and despair. Everything Max had given me, he took back: the house, the clothes, the jewelry. Well, everything but the STD, which thankfully was cleared up by antibiotics.

Let's pause here for one moment and consider the mess my life had become.

In today's society, it is not very popular to talk about God's laws and precepts. In fact, if the Caitlyn Jenner saga showed us anything, it's that society wants everyone to consider God's order as oppression. Facing it, changing it, challenging God's creation—and His established order—is considered brave and celebrated as "courageous." (ESPN controversially gave Jenner the ESPY award for courage, which raised a lot of eyebrows. Bob Costas, who didn't believe Jenner was the most deserving athlete, called it a "tabloid play.")

So let's get this straight, America.

Marriage, unborn babies, and even gender = oppressive.

Divorce, abortion, and surgical mutilation = emancipating.

But my own life—and probably yours—doesn't play out that way. In real life, getting married and staying married is a pathway to higher levels of financial stability and peace. In real life, having an abortion causes death, regret, and other health complications. In real life, you can't surgically enhance yourself to self-realization.

I thought that having sex outside of marriage would be fun and exciting. I thought that having an affair could be justified. After all, I didn't know he was married when it all started.

I thought that drugs wouldn't affect me, that I could still make good decisions and be healthy.

I didn't anticipate that these decisions would leave me worse than broke, emotionally devastated, and with a sexually transmitted disease.

Finally, I found a nice but small apartment that had two bedrooms and a doorman. I moved everything I owned to that house. I had 750 boxes of things. Gina, God bless her, did the best she could, but we couldn't walk through the hallways it was so crowded.

As we were standing in our new place, Lola and I—both at the same time—just broke down crying. I took her hand, led her into the bathroom, shut the door, and climbed into the bathtub. It was the only place free of boxes.

"I can't breathe here," she said.

"Me either."

We cried for twenty minutes, sitting in the tub in an apartment we'd never seen before. Finally, I was able to get a handle on my emotions.

"I promise you this," I said, clearing my throat. "Mama's gonna make this beautiful. This is gonna be all right. We're gonna be fine. We're gonna do it one room at a time, one day at a time."

And that's exactly what we did. Lola, Gina, and I unpacked each box and tried to make the apartment into yet another home. And there, while unpacking the boxes, I made a decision that would affect the rest of my life. No more men. For real this time. I was going to get work, take care of myself, and try to forge a path for Austin, Lola, and me that didn't rely on anyone else. I had no money, no job, and no agent. Because I was broken emotionally and broke financially, I couldn't do anything but call out to God. Finally. After all of those years sort of running away from God, I know He got my attention. This is when I went to Him and made a promise.

The author of Psalms wrote, "How I long for your precepts! Preserve my life in your righteousness."

We are living in a unique cultural moment. On every side, the society seems to be pushing our boundaries…telling us that God's laws and order are oppressive. That's why we must dig our feet into the ground and make the decision to believe in God's truth, not the culture's lies.

God has given us a choice. In fact, it's the same exact choice He's given all other cultures and all individuals. In Deuteronomy, God instructs: "I call heaven and earth to witness against you today, that I have set before you life and death, blessing and curse. Therefore choose life, that you and your offspring may live."

Now is exactly the time that Americans need to choose correctly. I was finally ready to try.

"Okay, God, I give up," I cried. "I surrender. Let's do it Your way from now on."

TWELVE

YOU SHALL TWEET THE TRUTH, AND THE TRUTH SHALL SET YOU FREE

*Truth, like gold, is to be obtained not by its growth,
but by washing away from it all that is not gold.*
—Leo Tolstoy, quoted in the *Wall Street Journal*

Now that I realized I was a conservative—and had been all along—I started paying more attention to politics. I was amazed at how Democrats and liberals made every single solitary thing about race. Every single thing. The common assumption was that *black people = Democrats*. Anything a white man or a Republican said was questioned as having some sort of racist undertone.

Once, while surfing the Internet, I saw what was described as a "gotcha" video that a liberal website filmed during a Romney junket, in which the candidate told a room full of white donors the following:

There are 47 percent of the people who will vote for
the president no matter what. All right, there are 47
percent who are with him, who are dependent upon
government, who believe that they are victims, who
believe the government has a responsibility to care for
them, who believe that they are entitled to health care,
to food, to housing, to you-name-it. That that's an
entitlement. And the government should give it to
them. And they will vote for this president no matter
what.... These are people who pay no income tax....
[M]y job is not to worry about those people. I'll never
convince them they should take personal responsibility
and care for their lives.

The liberal website presented this like it was the death knell
to his campaign. "Romney doesn't care about minorities," was
the spin. "Look what he says to a room full of white people when
he thinks minorities aren't watching!"

Only rarely did people actually deal with the substance of his
claim—that a large percentage of Americans are not paying taxes.
Was he right? CBS reported: "So is it true that 47 percent of Americans don't pay income tax? Essentially, yes, according to the Tax
Policy Center, which provides data showing that in 2011, 46.4
percent of American households paid no federal income tax."[1]

Of course, I only saw a snippet of Romney's speech that night,
so I don't know if he went on to talk about the fact that nearly
two-thirds of the no-income-tax-paying demographic do pay
some sort of payroll tax, or state, local, sales, and property taxes.

I don't know how he nuanced his claim, how he explained it. The liberal website released just enough to make him sound calloused. Even though the substance of what he said was right, he was being raked over the coals for being a white guy speaking the truth. I thought the "47 percent" comment was hilarious, as did everyone I know.

A few weeks later, I had gotten sick of all the conversation about Romney hating blacks. As a black woman, I decided to speak out. And, since it was 2012, I spoke out through my Twitter account—and inspired the Twitterstorm I told you about in chapter one.

Vote for Romney. The only choice for your future.

To my delight, the interview with Piers Morgan went really well, and I was very proud of how I did on the show. But here's the thing. After I came back home, I was still in the same situation.

"Gina, how much money do we have in the account?" I asked, which caused her to frown. "Just tell me."

"You have $100 in checking," she said. "Nothing in savings...or anywhere else." She kindly didn't mention that I also had overextended credit cards to the tune of $62,000. Plus, I owed the IRS. I tried not to think of it, but it's hard when you have to take care of yourself and kids.

I got a lot of Twitter hate over my Romney endorsement. But one day I got a letter about my tweet in the mail—an old-fashioned, handwritten letter written on actual paper. That got my attention.

"I just wanted you to know that what you did—endorsing Romney on Twitter—took a lot of guts." My eyes glanced down to the signature—Nathan, an attorney from Georgia, of all places. He had found my agent's name online and written me a letter. He went on to say that he had been a presidential candidate's chief of staff. "If you ever want to do politics for real, let me know."

I held the letter and bit my lip—was what he was saying a real possibility? Though I had never considered myself a political activist, I did like the idea of speaking my mind. In fact, the backlash made me more committed to speaking out. No one is going to silence me.

"Nathan, I got your letter, and wanted to thank you for sending it," I typed into my iPad. I went on to suggest that we keep in touch. A few months later, I got an e-mail from Nathan that would change the direction of my life.

"I'm going to be in Los Angeles for the Republican National Committee meeting," he said. "It will probably be boring—there ain't nothing cool about the Republican Party—but wanna come?"

I wasn't sure about the Committee meeting, but I was intrigued by this Southern lawyer who thought I had a future in—of all things—politics. We met at an Italian restaurant. At 6'2", his imposing presence was offset by his Southern accent and "aw shucks" persona. He told me about his wife, his three daughters, his suburban megachurch, and—of course—politics.

The Republican National Committee was a complete bore. We met the Party chairman and the head of minority outreach—a portly older white gentleman with a comb-over, who didn't know what to do with me. There were a lot of nervous white people telling me how they were going to reach black people in the next campaign cycle. I couldn't get a word in edgewise. There were even a few black people there—who really didn't want me there because, apparently, they liked being the only black people there.

I could tell that I didn't fit into anyone's mold—the Democrats', or even the Republicans'. I was just me. I was someone who had never read Edmund Burke, but knew that conservative principles worked in everyday life. I was—and am!—what most Americans are. I could immediately tell that the RNC was not going to be where I began the next chapter of my life. But I kept in touch with the Georgia attorney.

In fact, I began to rely on his judgment.

"Do you mind looking at this script?" Within the day, he'd respond with an "I'm no expert but this is stupid," or "Don't do this" comment.

Another project my agents gave me was a pseudo-reality show that attempted to convince people in a Southern small town that Jesus had come back.

"They want you to be like a newswoman?" Nathan asked me on the phone. I could hear the incredulity in his voice. "This is the dumbest thing I have ever seen. Who the hell is sending you this crap?"

"I need to fire this guy, Natey," I said. "Would you do it for me?"

He did. And after that I informed him that he was my manager. I heard a long silence on the other end of the phone and I heard him typing. "Natey, didn't you hear what I just said?"

"Yes," he replied. "I'm just Googling what the heck a 'manager' is."

He didn't know one thing about Hollywood, but he did know how to run political campaigns.

"Okay," he finally responded. "I'll run your campaign. But I don't know what I'm doing. This is your life."

"There is no format anymore. This is new territory. Plus, I trust you."

"That's your problem," Nathan said. "You need to stop trusting men. In fact, if you want me to be your manager, there is one condition. I am banning you from getting married for at least the next two years."

"What?" I asked, not believing that I heard him correctly.

"As far as I can tell, every bad financial and career decision you've made had to do with a man—particularly when you marry them," Nathan said. "You can look at this morally or you can look at this financially. But if you want me to work with you I'm banning you from getting married for the time being. You can have one date but not two."

I know it sounded unorthodox, but I couldn't argue. Men were my Achilles' heel.

After some rounds with some high-profile networks and producers, I could tell that Nathan had figured out Hollywood well enough to know that it wasn't brain surgery. It was basic human interaction. Even though he had a Southern drawl and a nice demeanor, they seemed to take him seriously enough. There were many amazing opportunities on my horizon, but they weren't happening fast enough.

"This is great for the future, but not for right now," he said of one job that arose. "It'll take a show two years to be in development and I need you to make money now."

I didn't quite understand how much financial pressure we were under. Without my knowledge, every month, Gina would call Nathan and tell him that we were out of money.

"What do we do?" Gina would ask him. "Stacey has no money for food."

When I would travel for work, everything would be paid for. However, the hotel always made me put down a credit card for "incidentals," in case I got something from the minibar or the hotel restaurants. Well, none of my credit cards worked, which put an immense amount of stress on me. It was frankly embarrassing that I'd gotten myself into such a financial predicament. I needed to start producing some income. In September, Nathan pulled me aside for a heart-to-heart. "I'm going to come up with a three-point plan and if I haven't done everything in a year I'm firing myself."

"Why would you do that?"

"If I can't show progress, you need someone else."

"I'm listening," I said.

"This is what we're gonna do," he said, holding up three fingers. "First, we're gonna get you paid for your opinion." He pointed to his first finger, and I laughed. I could totally imagine him laying down the law to his kids. Then, he touched his next finger. "Second, I'm going to make you the 'cool kid' again, so you can get back to acting." And finally he said, "Third, I'm going to figure out how to get you a book deal. Natey had started writing a speech about my life, and after about eight pages of single-spaced legal pad notes, he realized that this was more than just a speech.

"You think you can do all that?"

"If I can't, I don't deserve to be doing this. But first, pack your bags."

"Why?"

He had gotten frustrated with the Hollywood crowd.

"I'm taking you to New York."

"I can't afford bus fare," I said. "I sure as hell can't afford to go to New York."

Nathan rolled his eyes. "You're coming anyway." On his dime, we went to New York to meet with Roger Ailes, the legendary founding CEO of Fox News. Nathan had met him once after his duties with the presidential campaign he had run were over.

"Where are we staying?" I asked. Of course, Nathan was paying my way, so I had no right to be picky. But that didn't stop me.

"The Marriott Marquis in Times Square," he said. "It's right there, it's got a thousand rooms."

"We can't stay there!"

"Why on earth?" Nathan asked. I could tell he had no idea what it's like to be in New York and to have people recognize you.

"Trust me," I said. "I can't stay there."

We got a different hotel—one more used to dealing with people in the public eye. Nathan grumbled because it was more expensive, but soon he understood the necessity. I walked out of the hotel and there were already people waiting to take my photo. I walked straight back inside and got a "disguise"—simply a hat and shades…like all celebs in movies use.

"I'll need a car service too," I told Nathan, pointing to my five-inch heels.

"No way! It's one city block," he said. "Look, I got three daughters and a wife. I don't need this from you. Those are going in your purse. We're not doing a car service to accommodate your footwear."

In retrospect, he was right. I changed into comfy shoes for the walk and changed back when I got to the studio.

"No one else dares talk to her like that," Gina marveled, which caused us all to laugh.

"No one else dares call me Natey."

A month or two later, Nathan called me.

"I think we can check off number one."

"What are you talking about?"

"Roger Ailes just called me, and said, 'You're the guy who introduced me to Stacey, aren't you? What do you think she's doing?'"

I let out a scream of exuberance.

"Let me finish?" Nathan said.

"Talk faster!"

"Ailes, like me, saw the potential in you to really become an important voice in American culture."

I did a couple of shows a few times as a guest, and we had a deal by May. In four months, Nathan had already accomplished one-third of his stated goals.

On the day that I spent my very last dollar, the Fox check came.

God gives you what you need, when you need it.

An acting job came up in Florida.

"Miami?" I asked Nathan. "This week?"

"I'm not giving you a choice in this matter," Nathan said. "You're completely broke. This is a job. This is how capitalism works. You work, you get paid, you eat." Again, the lessons of life are conservative.

"I can't believe you get away with what you say to her," Gina mumbled.

"We're business partners. I make money if you make money, so this is how you make money. Until you've got cash flow, you'll do any legitimate job that's not immoral that pushes your career forward," he said.

I smiled.

"And by the way, you can go ahead and check off the second item on my list," he said.

Also, Samsung contacted us for permission to use a clip of *Clueless* in one of their commercials. Thankfully, they paid me a huge amount of money for it. I knew it was God—not Nathan, not even myself—Who was giving me opportunities to get back on my feet.

With money finally coming in, Nathan set me up with an accountant, advised me to be frugal—and how to cut costs!—and warned me that I had to start living differently. Thankfully, I have been well received at Fox and everyone is being very supportive and gracious. It is a welcome feeling to be appreciated, after so many people in my life have told me to keep my mouth shut.

"You're never gonna work in Hollywood again," I was told.

"You're black," my friends—and even family—told me. "Don't be a sellout."

Of course, when people tell me to shut up, that's when I'm most likely to speak.

After doing a few guest stints on Fox, I was offered a regular gig on *Outnumbered*. The show, in case you haven't seen it, is a talk show with four female panelists and one male panelist. They rotate the hosts so that there's always different chemistry in the dialogue about the day's events. I maintain my home in California but I fly into New York to do the shows. Some days I'm on Fox all day—on all kinds of shows offering all kinds of opinions. You might assume correctly that I am full of them, on virtually every topic. I love the whole experience. I love getting hair and makeup, I love going into the cold studio a little early so I can gather my thoughts, focus my mind, and get acclimated to the temperature before recording.

Our studio is located in the heart of the city, so pedestrians sometimes peek into the windows and wave in the hopes of getting on camera. I love all of the activity surrounding the topics of the day. To prepare for the show, we get a list of topics that might be covered. (That way, when a topic is brought up— whether it be about Iran, the First Lady's efforts to make everyone plant a garden, or the Oscars—our thoughts are organized and informed.) But we only get them two hours in advance. That quick turnaround took me a while to get used to. In fact, I'm still getting acclimated to the challenge. But with every show, I feel more and more confident, and I am growing more fascinated with the whole world of journalism and politics.

I love the hour preceding the airing. The other hosts talk to their friends and advisors about the topics before we go on.... "What do you think?" they might ask. There are disagreements, interesting give and take, and changes of opinion.

And that's *before* the cameras start rolling.

In the studio, people hand out coffee, the hosts look through their notes. Then, suddenly, the lights darken and the set gets quiet.

"Thirty seconds to the tease."

A couple of the hosts go live as they tell America what topics we'll be discussing that day. The excitement is palpable, I admit. Occasionally I get a little nervous. But I don't get as nervous as Nathan, who worries when I don't listen to his suggestions and just speak off the top of my head. If I catch his eye during the show after a rant, I can read his mind.

You just caused Twitter to explode again.

But that's the fun of it, right?

On a Thursday in April, I got a text from Natey telling me that Meredith Vieira had invited me on her show to discuss various topics. I love Meredith—not only is she a classy lady, the last time I was on her show I got to meet the sexy actor Anthony Mackie, who was promoting his upcoming movie, *Black or White.* Plus, Meredith and I have great chemistry. Of course I'd go.

I probably should've thought better of it. I had just had major surgery, from which I hadn't quite recovered. Or at least that's what my doctor would later tell me, when he was scolding me for taking the red-eye from Los Angeles to New York. I slept on the flight. When I arrived bright and early the next morning, I was happy to be in New York again. There's something about that city—my heart beats faster as soon as I see that skyline from my seat. I feel like a totally different person when I'm there. It's invigorating.

It was less invigorating when my greeter didn't show up for forty-five minutes, which caused me to have to lug my suitcases about a mile as I searched for him and the car. I could hear the sound of my doctor's voice telling me to take it easy, but I didn't want to miss out on Meredith's show. I went to my hotel, jumped in the shower, and went to NBC where I hurriedly got hair and makeup. I had gotten a list of topics we might discuss, and one of them was women's equality when it comes to pay. I didn't have to prepare for this topic. I knew beyond a shadow of a doubt what I was going to say. Don't make excuses because of your sex, your color, or your anything. That's where I'm coming from. Everyone has their own struggles. Life is hard, don't use anything as an excuse that'll hold you back. Nothing. I'm a woman. I'm black. I take full responsibility for my life. I don't care about statistics. I'll overcome them.

As I expected, it was wonderful to see Meredith. We chatted amiably, and I even told her (on air) that I'd decided not to have sex outside of marriage. Then the conversation turned to the supposed "wage gap" between men and women.

"It's an excuse. Stop making excuses," I said. "You know, if there are opportunities, seize them. And be prepared for them. And be the best, if that's what it takes. If you have to be extraordinary, then be extraordinary."

Meredith then quoted the "fact" that everyone in the media has been quoting for years. Women make 78 cents on the dollar that men make. Meredith said that, at this rate, her twenty-two-year-old daughter would finally live in a world of equal pay when she was in her sixties.

"I don't know if that's true…," I said.

"That's true, that's documented."

"…I feel like your daughter will be able to make as much money as she wants in her life. Just like you are. I mean, look at you…," I said.

"…I am successful," she said. "But it took a long time…. For many years I was not getting paid the same as the guys."

"And you think it's because you're a woman?"

"I think that had a lot to do with it…"

"…I guess I won't put my fate into anything other than my own action and taking my destiny in my, in my hands. I will not be victim to anything."

"I'm not saying I'm a victim. I'm pissed off. I don't wanna be a victim."

The crowd loved Meredith's outrage and began applauding. However, I wasn't buying it.

"If you want to be pissed off about it, then be pissed off about it and work harder for it. But I don't think us, you know, complaining about it, because there is a law passed that we get paid equal pay."

Meredith ended the show segment by saying, "Except we don't. But, we don't. We don't! We don't! We don't."

After the segment, we hugged. I love doing Meredith's show. She's never mean, and I enjoy the fun give-and-take about important issues. Meredith and I always agree to disagree. Everyone's entitled to their humble opinion, and I think she does a great job of keeping the conversation classy.

"So what did you guys talk about?" Nathan asked me when I called him on the way from the studio. I had to immediately catch a flight to Washington, D.C., which I'm sure my doctor would've hated...had he known.

"I told her I was no longer having sex outside of marriage," I said.

Nathan waited a beat. He didn't want to talk to me about my sex life or lack thereof. "Anything else?"

"Nothing really," I said.

That's why Nathan and I were both surprised when I started getting tweets about how "Meredith owned Stacey Dash on the wage gap issue!" I didn't feel like I'd gotten owned at all. Sure, I wish I had walked in there with more data about the truth behind the issue. But here's the thing. It's damn near impossible to find out the truth about any matter in American politics when the media tells lie after lie after lie. And even more than the media...the president of the United States regurgitated this myth during a State of the Union address.

"Today, women make up about half our workforce. But they still make 77 cents for every dollar a man earns," he said to America. "That is wrong, and in 2014, it's an embarrassment."

What's really an embarrassment is that President Obama must get his State of the Union talking points from MSNBC. This gender pay gap myth is the difference between the average earnings of all full-time men and women, without regard for differences in job choices, positions, schooling, tenure, or even how many hours they work per week. But that sure sounds like relevant data, right?

And so, like always, I went to Twitter to start speaking out.

> The so-called wage gap is mostly, and perhaps entirely, an artifact of the different CHOICES men and women make…

Then I linked to an article in *U.S. News & World Report* that pointed out that women are not "being cheated out of 24 percent of their salary." In fact, people get paid different amounts according to what they do with their lives—in what fields of study they choose to enroll, what types of professions they choose to pursue, what types of balances they choose to achieve between home and work life.

But I wasn't done on Twitter:

> I am not ANTI-WOMAN! I just don't believe that my gender needs a bunch of men in Congress to "save us" from the big bad world.

That one was retweeted several times. Then, I wrote:

#DashClass: Census data from 2008 show that single, childless women in their 20s now earn 8% more on average than their male counterparts.

And later:

The 77 cents vs a dollar is based on B.S. statistics. STOP USING IT. CELEBRATE that EDUCATED women in their 20s make more than men!

And

I DON'T CARE IF I AM THE LONE VOICE IN THE WOODS, I WILL NOT LET THE GOVERNMENT MAKE WOMEN AN ENTITLEMENT CLASS. #HOLDINGTHELINE

Okay, so maybe I was getting carried away with the all-caps, but this is a serious lie that the media has been spoon-feeding us for decades. Please. Then, to end things on a positive note—is that even a thing on Twitter?!—I tweeted:

.@meredithvieira is my friend. I LOVE having discussions w/ her on @MeredithShow. When we disagree it does not mean we are tense #GrownUps

I tweeted until the wee hours of the morning, going back and forth with naysayers, occasionally retweeting insults, and having just a generally good time. What an honor to be able to exercise my free speech rights while sitting in my bed, with my laptop, in my pajamas. I fell asleep, exhausted at all of the activity and the lingering effects of my surgery. The next day, I was shocked to wake up and discover that I had trended globally on Twitter.

I smiled.

It's amazing how big a punch you can deliver in 140 characters or less.

THIRTEEN

LOVE

Be patient with everyone, but above all with yourself.
Do not lose courage in considering your own imperfections
but instantly set about remedying them—every day
begin the task anew.

—St. Francis de Sales

G ina came through the door with the mail in her hand.

"You got a letter from the Bronx bureau president," she said, her eyes wide.

I tore open the letter and had to choke back the tears. "I've been invited to be inducted into the Bronx Walk of Fame."

"What does that mean?" Gina asked, grabbing the letter. She read aloud. "Members of the 2015 Walk of Fame class will be inducted during the 44th annual Bronx Week." She looked at me and explained. "Your name will be put on a street sign along Grand Concourse!"

"Get all the details, and reply now. Tell them I'll do whatever they want me to do," I said. "Oh and make sure you tell them that I'm deeply honored." I felt like God was giving me a second chance, sort of like how God is giving the Bronx a second chance. Did you know they've built the biggest mall in New York City in the Bronx? Yep. Crime has fallen, and real estate agents now have coined the term "SoBro" to make it a cool destination for New Yorkers. For years, my home neighborhood has been the nation's poorest congressional district. But now that Brooklyn and Queens neighborhoods have been built up—hipsterized!—people are looking at the South Bronx with fresh eyes.

I'm going to take my kids to my old neighborhood for the ceremony.

"Do you think my old building is still there?" I asked Gina.

"Why wonder?" she said, pulling up Google Maps. When I saw the street view of my old neighborhood, I started to shake and sob. There it was. My building, but there were no kids on the block like there used to be. Around it, I could see that some buildings had collapsed and others were boarded up. I felt like I'd gone back to a haunted house, even though I was just looking at it on the screen of my laptop from the comfort of California.

I can't imagine what I'm going to feel like when I'm actually there. I'm so thankful. I know what it is to be broke. I know what it is to have to strive and survive. I'm blessed enough that God granted me a job that I love to give me a second chance at life.

And speaking of love, about a year ago I was asked on *Outnumbered* a question that pertained to that topic. Some topics don't require any preparation, the kind I can talk about freestyle.

"Do you believe in love at first sight?" I was asked.

"Of course! It's the best kind."

I walked off the set, happy that I'd managed to pull off another great segment. Natey, however, was standing there with his hands on his head.

"Your take on love is the dumbest thing I've ever heard in my life," he said.

I laughed. Sometimes Natey is my manager, sometimes he's a friend, sometimes he's my enemy. I couldn't tell which was coming at me, so he took me to lunch to discuss my romantic deficiencies.

"Everything you just said about love makes no sense to me," Nathan said. "Not practically, not even biblically."

"What do you mean?" I asked.

"When you see a guy for the first time, do you see little blue birds flying around you like Cinderella?"

"Yes, and I see butterflies," I added.

"And you have your own soundtrack?"

Over the course of the lunch, he gave me a lecture on romance, but we also discussed how my views on romance were shaped—by my background. I grew up in circumstances where many girls got abused and most girls got pregnant too young with no husband and no money. Seventy-two percent of African American babies are being born to unmarried mothers.[1] Black families are split, and entire generations of black children are being raised without fathers.

"I guess you're right, Natey," I said, when I could finally get a word in edgewise. "I think my view of love is—" I struggled for the right word. "Warped."

"Well, it's what a teenage girl would say about love."

"It's fantasy," I said. "And I'll never stop believing in happily ever after anyway."

Sometimes on *Outnumbered*, they recycle the topics, depending on what's going on in the news. Last April I went to New York to do the show, went into the bowels of the Fox News building, and sat in the hair and makeup chair as I thought about the upcoming show. Right there, in my e-mail, I saw it in the list of topics.

"Do you believe in love at first sight?"

I smiled. When Nathan showed up a few minutes later, he eyed me suspiciously.

"What are you going to say this time?" he asked. "For real. You have a chance at a do-over."

"Which question?" I pretended I had no idea what he was talking about.

"The one about love at first sight."

"That I believe in it.... After all, my three marriages are proof!"

"Exactly," he laughed.

I was once again reminded of what a crazy world this is. After all of these years of bad romantic decisions, of giving myself to men who turned around and hurt me, I've decided to be celibate until marriage. I'm not going to continue doing the same thing over and over and expecting a different result.

I'm going to do things the way God intended.

Better late than never.

Oh and I guess I don't need to tell you that Nathan fulfilled the third item on the list, because you're holding it.

———

But here's the thing about love. While I might not quite get it when it comes to romantic love, I do understand love in a deep and profound way. I learned it when I held Austin in my arms in the hospital. When I saw Lola for the first time.

Her first word, by the way, was "Au-tin," and he's adored her ever since. Getting a new baby sister when he was thirteen was the best form of birth control I could have ever come up with for him. For a solid year, all Austin heard was "Go change her diaper. Go feed her. Go get her." He always did, mostly without complaining.

I know God gave me children for a reason. They are my everything. Lola is scary beautiful, kind, and loving. I tell her every single day—every single day—that I love her, that she can always tell me the truth, and that I'll always be there for her.

Recently, her father, Austin, and I went to a water park for her birthday with five of her friends. Austin came up and said, "These boys are shooting at them with water guns and trying to talk to them. It's freaking me out, Mom."

"Go take care of it," I laughed. "Go take care of it."

I may not have had success in my marriages, but I've definitely been blessed. As I watched Austin—my knight in shining armor—walk across the pool area to scare off the boys, I witnessed it. I understood it. I was almost overcome with it.

Love.

And that's just an echo of the love God has shown to me.

When I gave myself fully to God, things began happening that I never would have ever expected. Miraculous things. Who would've known a tweet that got such a negative response would turn out to be so positive for me? It made me realize that I had a voice, that I have something to say, and that what I say actually has value.

A Bible passage from Deuteronomy comes to mind:

"If you listen to these commands of the Lord your God that I am giving you today, and if you carefully obey them, the Lord will make you the head and not the tail, and you will always be on top and never at the bottom."

Most people where I come from don't know this verse. They don't dream. They don't think they have the right to even imagine a better way of life. They've been told it's impossible, which breaks my heart. If my message of faith, capitalism, and opportunity can reach just one person, then I feel like all the hate has been worth it.

And speaking of miraculous things, I recently got an invitation to the White House Correspondents' Dinner. When I told Natey, he flipped with excitement.

"That's amazing," he said.

"What is it?" I asked. I had never even heard of the event.

"Nerd Prom," Natey said, but the president and first lady and all kinds of senior government officials would be there, to be—supposedly—skewered by the media. "It's a multimillion-dollar week-long power trip, basically, and is one of the most coveted tickets in America."

"Should I go?"

"Of course!" he said, exasperated...as if I should have grasped the gravity of the invitation. But this is not my world. These are not my people. My career has been in Hollywood, not D.C. "It means you've made it," he added.

When he said those words, images of my life flashed before my face. Crying at the door when my parents left me with the family, stickball on the streets of the South Bronx, fights with kids who said I was stuck up, the rush of cold air as I jumped from my bedroom window, the adrenaline I felt as Richard Pryor and I watched our horse cross the finish line, the dread in the pit of my stomach when I couldn't afford to pay my electricity bills, the threats I received when people told me my thoughts as a black woman weren't welcomed...the fears that I'd be ostracized...that I'd never be successful if I espoused conservative views.

There goes my social life?

Not quite.

"Don't you see how amazing this is?" Natey said to me. "This whole adventure started with a tweet about voting for Romney, and now you get to go to dinner with the president."

As I got ready for the White House Correspondents' Dinner, I thought about how far this girl from the Bronx had come. I selected a long Dahlia dress that was emerald green with lace, rhinestones, and beads. (It had a train, so that when Brian

Kilmeade saw it later he called me a mermaid.) Yes, I brought out the five-inch heels for this, and Natey couldn't say a thing to me since he wasn't invited. I looked in the mirror, ran my hands over the beads and smiled. But then I heard it. My mother's voice.

You're not good enough. You're a tramp. Selfish. Stupid.

I shook my head, but the thoughts stubbornly lingered. I should've been so excited about the moment, but the thoughts in my head from my mother effectively popped the bubble.

I got in the shower and tried to wash her out of my head.

God shows His love for us in that while we were still sinners, Christ died for us.

If that sacrifice was made for me, then I'm not worthless. In fact, my life has infinite worth. Because it was given to me, it can't be taken away. Especially not by my mom.

I toweled off, trying to think about my worth and my value. By the time I walked out the door, I felt proud of being in this position and worthy of the invitation.

The dinner was held at the ballroom of the Washington Hilton Hotel, the infamous location of the assassination attempt on Ronald Reagan. When I arrived, completely made up and ready for this "event of the year," I was stopped at the door.

"Ticket?" one of the event staffers asked me.

"I don't have a ticket." Apparently, the people at Fox were supposed to hand me a paper ticket, a fact I learned too late.

"You can't get in without a ticket," he said. "Go to the concierge and see if they have yours." The concierge didn't have it either, so I paced back and forth in the lobby, texting Natey and trying—desperately—to figure out how to get into that room.

As I fretted, people would stop me and say, "Are you Stacey Dash? Can I get a photo?" I'd pause, strike a pose, and smile. This, in a way, encapsulated how I've often felt about my life in general: that it looked good, but was a façade. That someday someone was going to look at me and say, "You're a fraud. We see you for what you are now."

As I paced back and forth in that lobby, I wondered...would that be today? Maybe my mom had been right about me the whole time.

Thankfully, mercifully, the other Fox News guests arrived. They embraced me, put their arms around me, and brought me right into the grand ballroom.

I felt a little like the people described in a biblical parable about a man who gave a great feast. He told his servant, "Go out quickly into the streets and alleys of the town and bring in the poor, the crippled, the blind and the lame.... Go out to the roads and country lanes and compel them to come in, so that my house will be full."

No, I wasn't poor, crippled, blind, or lame. But I could just as easily imagine the Bible saying, "go out quickly into the streets and bring in the drug addicts, the abandoned children, the rape victims, and the unwanted." That's how God does things. That's what He has done for me.

That night, I sat with the Fox personalities on the right hand side of the room, and the president of the United States sat next to the podium at the front of the ballroom. There, a comedienne stood and threw jokes at the president, at the most powerful man in the world. And he laughed. In many countries, people who criticize their leaders end up dead, especially women. As much as I disrespect Obama's policies, I had to smile...at a world leader who subjects himself to such a spectacle. But also at a country that makes it possible for a black kid from the South Bronx to end up in the same room with a black kid who ended up being president. Also, I smiled at how people in our democracy get along in spite of profound political disagreements, at how Americans at their best esteem free speech above all else...above politeness and political correctness.

May my story encourage all Americans—no matter their color, sex, background, or political persuasion—to gather up the small amount of courage it takes to open their mouths and use the liberty purchased for us with blood.

Sure, it might impact your social life. But it also might take you places you never dreamt possible.

ACKNOWLEDGMENTS

I never knew how much went into making a book!

A big thanks to these people for making my first literary experience so much fun: Regnery publisher Marji Ross and editor in chief Harry Crocker; Elizabeth Kantor, my wonderful editor; Maria Ruhl, my excellent copy editor; John Caruso, for the great jacket design; Henry Pereira, who made the pages look good; Deborah Anderson, for a cover photo I love.

And to my collaborator Nancy French, for believing in my story and helping me tell it.

I'd also like to thank my agent Chris Park for her hard work finding just the right home for this book. I couldn't have done it without you.

A big thank you to Gina Benavidez, who takes care of everything—you are like family to me.

To Patrick, for making this possible.

To Austin and Lola, for showing me what love looks like. I love you more than you will ever know—you've made my life complete.

NOTES

THREE: WHY BLACK PEOPLE SHOULD VOTE REPUBLICAN EVERY TIME

1. Steve Berman, "ESPN's Stephen A. Smith: Why Every Black
    Person in America Should Vote Republican for 1 Election," BizPac
    Review, March 19, 2015, http://www.bizpacreview.com/2015
    /03/19/espns-stephen-a-smith-why-every-black-person-in-america-
    should-vote-republican-for-1-election-188128; see also Trent
    Baker, "ESPN's Stephen A. Smith: For One Election, Every Black
    Person Should Vote Republican," Breitbart, March 18, 2015,
    http://www.breitbart.com/video/2015/03/18/espns-stephen-a-
    smith-for-one-election-every-black-person-should-vote-
    republican/.

FIVE: THE DECISION MAKER

1. Drug Policy Alliance, "Drug War Statistics," no date, http://www.drugpolicy.org/drug-war-statistics.
2. Matt Taylor, "The War on Weed: Still Expensive, Racist, and Failed," Vice, June 4, 2013, http://www.vice.com/read/the-war-on-weed-still-expensive-racist-and-failed.
3. Emily Badger, "The Meteoric, Costly, and Unprecedented Rise of Incarceration in America," *Washington Post*, April 30, 2014, http://www.washingtonpost.com/news/wonkblog/wp/2014/04/30/the-meteoric-costly-and-unprecedented-rise-of-incarceration-in-america/.
4. Tygen Tsai and Paola Scommegna, "U.S. Has World's Highest Incarceration Rate," Population Reference Bureau, August 2012, http://www.prb.org/Publications/Articles/2012/us-incarceration.aspx.

SIX: EDUCATION, THE GREAT INTEGRATOR

1. "Youth More Likely to Be Bullied at Schools with Anti-Bullying Programs, UT Arlington Researcher Finds," University of Texas Arlington News Center, September 12, 2013, https://www.uta.edu/news/releases/2013/09/jeong-bullying.php; Allie Bidwell, "Study: Anti-Bullying Programs May Have Opposite Effect," *U.S. News & World Report*, September 13, 2013, http://www.usnews.com/news/articles/2013/09/13/study-anti-bullying-programs-may-have-opposite-effect.
2. Ibid.
3. "A Playbook for the Youngest Learners: Educators and Policymakers Work to Assure a Strong Start and Sustained Momentum from Preschool Onward," *Education Week*, January 2, 2015, http://www.edweek.org/ew/articles/2015/01/08/a-playbook-for-the-youngest-learners.html?intc=EW-QC15-LFTNAV.

4.   Reid Wilson, "Education Spending Balloons, but Students in Some States Get More Money than Others," *Washington Post*, January 26, 2014, http://www.washingtonpost.com/blogs/govbeat/wp/2014/01/26/education-spending-balloons-but-students-in-some-states-get-more-money-than-others/.

5.   "The Nation's Report Card: Trends in Academic Progress 2012," National Center for Education Statistics, June 2013, http://nces.ed.gov/nationsreportcard/pubs/main2012/2013456.aspx.

6.   Philip Elliot, "Study: US Education Spending Tops Global List," Associated Press, June 25, 2013, http://bigstory.ap.org/article/study-us-education-spending-tops-global-list.

7.   Erika Johnsen, "The DOJ Drops Its Suit against Louisiana's School Voucher Program, Kind Of. Not Really," Hot Air, November 19, 2013, http://hotair.com/archives/2013/11/19/the-doj-drops-its-suit-against-louisiana-school-choice-program-kind-of-not-really/.

8.   Hollie McKay, "Stacey Dash: The Obama Administration Is 'A Bunch of Bullies,'" Fox News, September 27, 2013, http://www.foxnews.com/entertainment/2013/09/27/stacey-dash-obama-administration-is-bunch-bullies/.

9.   W. Bradford Wilcox and Elizabeth Marquardt, "The State of Our Unions 2010: When Marriage Disappears," The National Marriage Project at the University of Virginia and the Center for Marriage and Families at Institute for American Values, 2010, http://stateofourunions.org/2010/SOOU2010.php.

10.   Fifty-four percent of all births to never-married women between fifteen and fourty-four years old. Ibid.

11.   Nick Schulz, *Home Economics: The Consequences of Changing Family Structure* (AEI Press, 2013), 17.

12.   Jason L. Riley, "Race Relations and Law Enforcement," *Imprimis* 44 (January 2015): 1, http://imprimis.hillsdale.edu/race-relations-and-law-enforcement/.

13. Ibid.

14. Eduardo Porter, " A Simple Equation: More Education = More Income," *New York Times*, September 10, 2014, http://www. nytimes.com/2014/09/11/business/economy/a-simple-equation-more-education-more-income.html.

15. "11 Facts about Education and Poverty in America," DoSomething. org, no date, https://www.dosomething.org/facts/11-facts-about-education-and-poverty-america.

16. "Earnings and Unemployment Rates by Educational Attainment," Bureau of Labor Statistics, April 2, 2015, http:// www.bls.gov/emp/ep_chart_001.htm.

17. Katie Furtick, "Annual Privatization Report 2014: Education," Reason Foundation, April 2014, http://reason.org/files/apr-2014-education.pdf.

18. Greg Foster, "A Win-Win Solution: The Empirical Evidence on School Choice," Friedman Foundation for Educational Choice, April 13, http://www.edchoice.org/wp-content/uploads/2015 /07/2013-4-A-Win-Win-Solution-WEB.pdf.

19. Ibid.

20. "Teachers Union Exposed: Protecting Bad Teachers," Center for Union Facts, 2015, http://teachersunionexposed.com/protecting. php.

21. "Use of Dues for Politics," Center for Union Facts, 2015, https:// www.unionfacts.com/article/political-money/.

SEVEN: THE POWER OF FAMILY

1.   Nancy A. French, "New Study: Casual Sex Depresses Teens, Raises Risk of Suicide," Rare, December 3, 2013, http://rare.us/ story/new-study-casual-sex-depresses-teens-raises-risk-of-suicide/#2zZu2hCdxKW5TKmi.99.

EIGHT: SEARCHING FOR A FAIRY TALE

1. "American Community Survey, 2007–2009," U.S. Bureau of the Census, athttp://factfinder2.census.gov/faces/tableservices/jsf/pages/productview.xhtml?pid=ACS_09_3YR_S1702&prodType=table, from Robert Rector, "Marriage: America's Greatest Weapon against Child Poverty," The Heritage Foundation, September 5, 2012, http://www.heritage.org/research/reports/2012/09/marriage-americas-greatest-weapon-against-child-poverty#_ftn1.

2. James Alan Fox and Richard Moran, "Sex Assault Surveys Not the Answer: Column," *USA Today*, August 10, 2014, http://www.usatoday.com/story/opinion/2014/08/10/sexual-assault-rape-survey-college-campus-column/13864551/; Christopher P. Krebs, Christine H. Lindquist, Tara D. Warner, Bonnie S. Fisher, and Sandra L. Martin, "The Campus Sexual Assault (CSA) Study: Final Report," Department of Justice, December 2007, https://www.ncjrs.gov/pdffiles1/nij/grants/221153.pdf.

3. Christina Hoff Somers, "5 Feminist Myths That Will Not Die," *Time*, September 2, 2014, http://time.com/3222543/5-feminist-myths-that-will-not-die/.

4. Ibid.

5. Katie Sanders, "Mika Brzezinski Repeats Myth That Super Bowl Sunday Has 'Highest Rate of Domestic Violence,'" PolitiFact, September 18, 2014, http://www.politifact.com/punditfact/statements/2014/sep/18/mika-brzezinski/mika-brzezinski-repeats-myth-super-bowl-sunday-has/.

NINE: LIFE AND DEATH

1. "History," Colt Manufacturing, 2015, http://www.colt.com/Company/History.aspx/.

2. Michael A. Memoli, "Eric Holder: Gun Lobby 'Simply Won' by Killing Sandy Hook Reforms," *Los Angeles Times*, February 8, 2015, http://www.latimes.com/nation/politics/politicsnow/la-pn-holder-guns-20150208-story.html.

3.   David French, "My Family's Safety Is More Important than San
      Francisco's Crazy Gun Laws," *National Review*, June 10, 2015,
      http://www.nationalreview.com/article/419572/san-francisco-gun-
      laws?target=author&tid=1048.

TWELVE: YOU SHALL TWEET THE TRUTH, AND THE TRUTH SHALL SET YOU FREE

1.   "Who Doesn't Pay Federal Taxes?," Tax Policy Center, no date,
      http://www.taxpolicycenter.org/taxtopics/federal-taxes-
      households.cfm.

THIRTEEN: LOVE

1.   Jesse Washington, "Blacks Struggle with 72 Percent Unwed
      Mothers Rate: Debate Is Growing inside and outside the Black
      Community on How to Address the Rising Issue," NBC News,
      November 7, 2010, http://www.nbcnews.com/id/39993685/ns/
      health-womens_health/t/blacks-struggle-percent-unwed-
      mothers-rate/#.VUpuxxPF-rw.